MAILING LIST STRATEGIES
A GUIDE TO DIRECT MAIL SUCCESS

ROSE HARPER
**President and Chief Executive Officer
The Kleid Company Inc.**

MCGRAW-HILL BOOK COMPANY

NEW YORK   ST. LOUIS   SAN FRANCISCO
AUCKLAND   BOGOTÁ   HAMBURG
LONDON   MADRID   MEXICO   MONTREAL
NEW DELHI   PANAMA   PARIS   SÃO PAULO
SINGAPORE   SYDNEY   TOKYO   TORONTO

DEDICATION

To my husband, Ron, for his constant and unfailing encouragement and for his support throughout our life together. To Lewis Kleid, who gave me the extraordinary opportunity to function as an entrepreneur. We worked so well together. To the many friends I've made throughout the years in our business—you very special people know who you are. To my devoted staff for their loyalty and dedication to our company. To the direct mail discipline which never lost the challenge of constant learning. And also to our pets, Macke and Jacke and Terri and Berry, who were disciplined enough to stop eating my words after they ate part of the first chapter.

Library of Congress Cataloging-in-Publication Data

Harper, C. R. (C. Rose)
    Mailing list strategies.

    Includes index.
    1. Mail-order business.   I. Title.
HF5466.H33   1986   658.8'72   85-23132
ISBN 0-07-026675-1

    567890   DOC/DOC   89321098

ISBN 0-07-026675-1

The editors for this book were William Sabin and Marci Nugent, the designer was Dennis Sharkey, and the production supervisor was Teresa F. Leaden. It was set in Baskerville by The Saybrook Press, Inc.

Printed and bound by R. R. Donnelley & Sons, Inc.

CONTENTS ████████████████████

CHAPTER 8
INFORMATION: A MIRROR TO THE FUTURE 101

CHAPTER 9
LIST TESTING: SCIENCE OR ART? 129

CHAPTER 10
INTERNAL FILES: A HIDDEN ASSET 161

PREFACE

I was prompted to prepare this book by my frequent encounters with a lack of understanding of the importance of the mailing list in direct mail marketing and the analytical measurements which are so crucial to success. Perhaps "the list" didn't meet response expectations, but isn't it important to explore why? What is learned from the successes and failures provides a continuum of the critical information required for direct mail planning.

Sure, there are more uncertainties than absolutes in direct mail marketing. However, the more we capitalize on the measurement capabilities of direct mail, the faster we will move toward a meeting between the uncertainties and the absolutes.

There are several people to whom I would like to express my appreciation for helping prepare the manuscript for this book:

Marcel Tyszler of Marcel Tyszler Associates, Los Angeles, California, for his input on the statistical theories and applications in Chapter 9.

Nat Ross, who read my original manuscript and gave me much encouragement.

Ingrid Carey, my long-time assistant, who had to process the words through the word processor over a burdensome period of time. As we all know, a lot of writing is rewriting. Ingrid never complained. For that, I am so grateful.

And how can I forget our industry, which provided me with the challenges of learning over three decades? I can't. It's been for me an enormously gratifying experience to be in a business discipline where you never can presume to know all the answers.

Rose Harper

Without Customers There Is No Business

The selection of the lists to be used in a direct mail campaign must follow a logical path just like any other business decision-making process. And defining this process will result not only in more successful direct mail campaigns but also in marketing planning, which is a process, not just a sales forecast or a budget. Marketing planning must be a cohesive and ongoing process dedicated to attracting new customers and retaining the present ones. The fact is that, no matter what business you're in, *you are in the customer business.*

For many (if not all) direct marketing companies, the customer file is not only a significant asset but also a marketing-decision support system. From in-depth analysis of who the customers are, what they need, why they buy, and what they buy, new insights can be gained into customer motivation, buying behavior, product acceptance, new product development, etc. And, equally important, this information will lead to tactical targeting in the new-customer acquisition process. As we all know, any business needs a steady diet of *new* customers to stay healthy. Why? To replace lost customers, to keep in touch with the marketplace, and to maintain a steady profit level.

THE NAME OF THE GAME

Think about the name of our game, which is "direct marketing" and in this book "direct mail." If we were 100 percent efficient and productive, our mailings would go exclusively to people who *want* to receive them. We're a long way from that goal because in direct mail we are also dealing with mathematical chance. However, the more we understand, analyze, evaluate, and then project our direct mail campaigns, the better we're going to do. And in this process the selection of lists is critical; much of the success (or failure) of a direct mail campaign rests on the *mailing list*. The more we know in advance, the lower our risk.

THE NAMES ON THE LIST

The names and addresses on a mailing list consist of a group of consumers or businesses all having one or more things in common. This meaningful group is important in direct mail, which involves sending a sales proposition to considered prospects. The objective, of course, is to elicit a positive response to the mailing and to convert the prospect into a customer. On this basis, it is easy to understand that the list is of significant value in the direct mail equation.

If you send your message to the right prospect, your chances that the mailing package will be opened and read are very high: about 75 percent according to research surveys conducted during the past several years. No other medium can promise that intensity factor—and bear in mind that lists are at the very center of your direct mail strategy.

THOUSANDS AND THOUSANDS OF LISTS

There are literally thousands of lists available that cover every conceivable market you might be interested in reaching. Within each list, there are segments that can be selected on the basis of geographic, demographic, behavioral, and other discriminants. So how do you logically select those lists which appear to have the most chance for success? It all starts with an understanding of your product or service as it relates to the list marketplace based on demographic, psychographic, and a host of other attributes. In other words, you begin with a market potential analysis.

With the market potential analysis, then, the selection of lists must be viewed from a perspective within the integrative concept of a direct mail campaign, which can be one large rewarding puzzle with a dynamic intermix of copy, offer, price, fulfillment, support media, and *lists*. To stay in control, direct marketers must view every mailing as a test which must be measured and analyzed to a point where the data collection can lead to conclusions, knowledge, and direction for decision making.

THE MONOTONY OF UNIFORMITY

It's time that direct marketers get out of the "sea of sameness." With all the competition that exists now and that is still growing, it will take a high degree of creativity on all fronts to make your promotions rewarding. It is essential, too, that marketers recognize that the key to direct mail success is the proper balance of consistency and innovation. After all, we certainly want to profit from our experience and not ignore what has worked in the past, nor exclude the new directions brought on by demographic and psychographic upheavals that have and will continue to reshape American markets.

For example, too often you hear that "the list doesn't work" when in fact the creative message did not address the real and perceived needs of the people on the list. It is important that marketers respond to the fact that the target does not stand still. In other words, marketers should be ready to change the promotional appeal and possibly the product itself to meet contemporary needs.

The companies in direct marketing which have increased profits in a very competitive environment have done so by using information systems in linking with customers. This practice helped these companies to differentiate their products and services and their customers. They individualized their customer by analysis of the when and how, the what and why, and the where and who and thereby created a methodology for spotting opportunities.

One concrete example (from *The Direct Marketing Handbook*, 2d ed., 1986, written by Edward L. Nash, President BBDO Direct, Inc., published by McGraw-Hill) is *Consumer Reports*, a consumer magazine that ranks efficiency of products related to costs and other important factors. Traditionally, *Consumer Reports* used only male lists, on the theory that only males were involved in the purchases (refrigerators, automobiles, etc.) which required a buying guide. A change in emphasis of the copy appeal to food orientation made lists of females equally successful and enabled the *Consumer Reports* list universe to double in size. Eventually the editorial content followed suit and included more articles of the type that seem to appeal to the broader universe. This is a perfect example of a blend of marketing imagination and instinct which resulted in market expansion, which is critical to all businesses. And it also enforces the message put out by a financial services company: "After an in-depth study of our markets and products, it became clear that the future emphasis must be on what our customer needs and demands and not what a financial services company wishes to offer."

INFORMATION: THE NEW PRIORITY

Data gathering is pivotal in the path to understanding present customers and potential customers. Even the most sophisticated research design cannot offset poor information. In developing information systems, you must acquire an understanding of the data needed for in-depth analysis. This necessitates the maximization of the *quality* of the data and not just the quantity. Evaluating the performance of lists requires accurate and continual feedback to sharpen target effectiveness. It's a matter of research, statistics, and mathematical techniques synchronized to meet the criteria on which list decisions can be based with a supportive level of confidence.

A WAY OF THINKING

All of this will lead to market consciousness, that is, a way of thinking that relates to people and a way of thinking built on qualified and quantified experience, leading to an understanding of the psychology of when, why, and who buys and why some buy more than others. It is also reasonable to assume that from internal files it is possible to acquire information from *your* market niche to supplement the information available about markets in general. These analytical disciplines will uncover the societal trends and patterns that will influence the judicious use of lists.

A major stumbling block on the road to successful direct mail promotions is a lack of information—good, fundamental information—on which to base decisions. Very often information reflects past trends rather than future needs. Today, however, as we face increasing change and volatility, there are lessons for us to learn from the past while keeping in mind that information should be a mirror to the future. The future will belong to direct marketers who are armed with a multidimensional system of information, that is, better data, which lead to better profits, which lead to a better future.

This book concentrates on those factors important to the successful usage of direct mail marketing with the emphasis on lists—the cement which keeps the building blocks together.

CHAPTER 1

Direct Mail: The Personal Medium

That people buy by mail is beyond dispute. The reasons are as varied as the products sold, with the most emphasis on *convenience*. In many of the surveys conducted over the years, there appears to be a great deal of ambivalence about receiving advertising mail. On the surface, many will deny any interest and/or criticize its value. But when prodded further, their attitudes reveal basic contradictions. They admit that they open the mail to look at it and frequently make use of it by: redeeming the coupons, subscribing to magazines, joining book or record clubs, purchasing merchandise, taking out insurance, and contributing to charitable causes.

To capsulize the findings in these surveys, while "attitude" very often did not correspond to "activity," the most critical and distinct corollary emerging between receptivity and activity was the type of product or service being offered. It is a combination of the right product with the right message to the target prospect that appears to count. This suggests that mail campaigns must be designed to achieve the required results with the smallest total mailing quantity. Thus targeted marketing is a business necessity.

After years of shotgun marketing, direct mail entered a new frontier and perhaps started to come of age in 1967. The catalyst? Zip codes. At that time everyone complained about the costs. The costs were certainly there and fixed, but the return on investment is still accruing. It seems fair to call this step, forced on the industry, a major thrust into technology which led direct mail, and indeed all the channels of direct marketing, to a higher level of sophistication.

This new phase was the key to the growth of direct marketing—the key that enabled direct marketing to command an increasingly higher share of the total advertising dollars spent in the United States. The advertising community became aware of the power of direct marketing along with many of the *Fortune* 500.

This push into technology for an industry (particularly mail order) that had been around for a long time and was to some degree mature was the catalyst which enabled companies to become information-driven. This intelligence is being used by the technologist and the direct marketing manager in determining business direction, product development, and innovative marketing techniques. Mail order, after all, was started by an innovator, Aaron Montgomery Ward, who recognized the opportunity to expand his marketplace via mailing a two-page flyer to prospective customers based on where they lived. Information is an energy force that can't be ignored.

In developing any information system, there are obviously many strategic options. In direct marketing, the focus of the system must be on the customer and prospect. The strategic target must be the search for new and more definitive means of counting and describing customers and prospects. If the system is undernourished in this aspect, accountability will suffer. If we consider direct mail a personal medium, the system's advantage must come from segmentation capabilities.

Segmentation is the path to dividing and understanding your buying public—by age, income, gender, tastes, and preferences—and then to correlating these attributes into a viable market and to targeting products at each grouping with great precision.

Just 3 decades ago, there were approximately 300 lists available but not too many mailers. So, every competent list broker and every successful mailer manually analyzed the effects of certain patterns of human behavior, knowledge of seasonal trends, and such intangibles as the economic ambience and financial constraints. These variables were then integrated into the development of a mail plan.

Direct mail practitioners were using, in a mathematical sense, covariance, but without realizing it. Covariance isn't easy to explain.[1] *Variance*

---

1. The mathematical definition of "covariance" is the product of the standard deviations of two given variables and the coefficient of correlation between them.

means the "state, quality, or facts of being variable, different." *Co-*, as a mathematical prefix, means "complement of." We're talking about the variables just mentioned which are measured with respect to one another in accordance with a fixed mathematical relationship. But this procedure was used instinctively. Today, the electronic brains can produce this information in seconds.

Always bear in mind that consumers are purposeful human beings with goals. They set their goals both on their own and on suggestions from others. Direct mail can be a powerful persuader if the right message is sent to the right prospect at the right price. And this requires a constant awareness of the socioeconomic forces which are splintering the marketplace. Your marketplace.

SPLINTERING MARKETS

Today's changing marketplace can be compared to the shifting patterns of a kaleidoscope. Trend watchers observe and confirm an increasing diversity in consumer lifestyles which were sparked by three major demographic trends: women in the work force, two-income families (the norm now, and not the exception, with women bringing in 40 percent of the family income), and smaller households. Consumers are growing increasingly different from one another. There's a tremendous change in progress relative to attitudes, living arrangements, and family composition.

For example, a little over 3 decades ago 70 percent of all households were made up of a father who worked full time outside the home, a mother who worked full time inside the home, and two or more children of school age. Today this type of household represents only 14 percent. In addition, more and more people are exercising their options regarding marriage and children. As a result, single-person households and households without children are as common today as the households with children were earlier.

In the 1950s, the majority of the population had achieved only a grade school education, but the "baby-boomers," born between 1946 and 1964, changed that. Now, 1 out of every 3 persons in the United States is a baby-boomer, which according to the latest statistics amounts to 75 million people. Most have formed a population segment with high education and have influenced the emerging "affluent society." This population cluster has led the growing demand for products and services that offer more value for the dollar. These trend setters are interested in products for their health and physical fitness, home environment, electronics, leisure activities, and money and financial management. These consumers are the "wired-up" population and represent the core buyers of video cameras, cassette players, and personal computers.

Audiences are splintering as they seek more and more specialized information and products. It is the responsibility of direct marketing managers to identify the "splinters." Over the next decade, the consumer will have a staggering assortment of media options as will the advertiser. This will result in the ability to reach smaller, pinpointed audiences.

Keeping your customer and potential customer in focus involves a constant awareness of the changing texture of American society. Societal changes and national consciousness affect a wide range of decisions for people: how they work, play, shop, think, keep warm, and keep cool, where they live, what they read, and a host of other things.

Doesn't all of this explain the pervasive move toward segmentation? What is speeding this revolution? Technology which makes it possible to identify segments and to respond to their particular needs. But all this fine-tuning and targeting has other implications. How do you reliably measure these small segments on a valid basis? With more sophisticated analytical systems and with the combined efforts of marketers, researchers, mathematicians, and technologists—efforts that result in a blending of art and science.

The strategic "room" for direct marketers in the next decade and beyond will be the data processing room. Here will be the opportunity to subdivide customers and prospective customers by purchasing behavior and lifestyle. Here will be the opportunity for product differentiation, new product development, and personalized promotions. Here will be the opportunity to set up a store for each customer, a store that never closes.

MEDIA OPTIONS (QUANTIFICATION)

Today's direct marketers don't make their offers exclusively through the mail. There are other important and supportive direct marketing streams: space, broadcast, co-ops, package and billing inserts, phone, interactive cable TV, syndication, third-party endorsements, co-op response decks, etc. The task of the direct marketers, simply stated, is to promote their products to customers and prospects in the most productive manner. In this pursuit, direct marketers must seek the medium or combination of media most efficient for their product or service. The acquisition and retention of customers is the road every business must take to accomplish its sales and growth objectives.

Let's look at this scenario. A publisher develops a subscription promotion of 2 million names. The cost of the list, printing, mailing services, and postage approximates 30 cents per piece. A response of 1 percent (20,000) would result in a cost per subscriber of $30. In terms of the publisher's economics, this is not an acceptable cost. Enter the "what-if" game. If there were proven selections which would make it possible to mail 1,500,000 names from the same lists at a return of 1.2 percent (18,000), the order cost would immediately be reduced by $5 and the total promotion cost by $150,000. This saving affords the publisher the option of allocating these funds to other subscription acquisition channels. Regardless of the original marketing strategy, it is important to recognize that media patterns have changed and perhaps so has the concept of a "base" medium. In this example, if you were the publisher, you would be forced to examine all the possible media and decide on how much to spend and where. You would have to use the principle of complementarity.

FORECASTING: SCIENCE OR ART?

Direct mail marketing is complex and multifaceted—and also measurable and effective. Direct mail marketers must view every mailing as a *test* of accountability.

Anyone who has had to forecast knows that the chances of being wrong are always present. This is true of economic forecasts, weather forecasts, and sales forecasts. But even with the possibility of error, the main reason to forecast is to reduce risk by applying and using every available bit of information to anticipate the most probable outcome.

Since computers became part of company life, the accuracy of sales forecasting has increased dramatically. Computer technicians, statisticians, and mathematicians have come up with an impressive array of new techniques. Therefore, sales forecasting has become much more scientific in the past 2 decades along with the recognition that there is no universal methodology which can be used by every company. But the art part, i.e., good management judgment based on intuition and experience, has not disappeared. It's the bridge over the flowing river of information.

Projecting a direct mail campaign means anticipating what is likely to happen by determining which elements will most likely influence the outcome. Planning is not successful only because someone is a "good planner." If unqualified information and unrealistic assumptions are used to develop the plan, the outcome will speak for itself.

With technology as our partner, it is possible to develop the identifiers which have clear implications for the direct mail plan: socioeconomic trends, seasonality, pricing, product acceptance, evaluation of previous promotions, geodynamics, and a host of other factors. In order to predict response, a constant process of monitoring the integrity of the information system must be in place. A straightforward, disciplined, systematic process greatly influences the factors of risk reduction. (Even a gambler in Las Vegas acknowledges the benefits of reducing risk.) It is essential to develop a plan that lets you analyze and measure results accurately relative to objectives, a plan that will provide substantive data base information for future planning. Historical perspectives can and do provide key direction. The future can always use some advice from the past.

LIST DEVELOPMENT PROGRAM

Selecting responsive lists is a development program that creates real economic value for the user. It is, or should be, a fundamental goal for all direct mail managers. But the technique for accomplishing this strategem is not a science or perhaps even an art. Extensive testing has been the answer.

But the testing can and must be controlled. While you can't ignore the opportunities of list testing, results should be direct and measurable. Knowledge of the characteristics of mail lists (response rates, costs, conversion rates, nonpay rates, and seasonal and geographic attributes) is essential in the continuing information stream. Direct mail planning must be viewed as a continuing process, not a one-shot effort each time a mailing happens.

But this "research" (as you will see as we go along in this book) needs to be synthesized into the results-oriented concept of the "sum of the parts" rather than "a list is a list." There really is no *neutral* element in direct mail; all are interactive.

Direct mail has been (and still is) so powerful a medium that response can cover up a high degree of error. But the more we recognize which elements impact most forcibly on response, the better we're going to do. We can't sit still and always play it safe. *Analogy:* Take a boat. Any boat. You can achieve placidity only by letting it drift downstream. If you anchor it, the current, however mild, will set up ripples against the bow: This is known as "making waves." If you want to navigate upstream, you have to make a really massive investment of energy, whether you paddle a canoe or pay for the Diesels.

Our "boat" is information. Our objective is predictive and focused marketing. With high select, high tech, high touch, high math, we have the opportunity, with high response, to sell directly more goods and services than any of us ever dreamed of. If, and it's a very high if, we understand how to use the tools of our trade and—in direct mail particularly—*lists.*

CHAPTER 2

Service Companies: Interactive Disciplines

There are several types of companies with special skills which are important to the direct mail process. Even though in some instances there are competitive aspects, these professionals work together cooperatively with common goals: the advancement of the art and science of direct mail marketing for the benefit of the mailer and the list owner.

LIST BROKERS

A *list broker* is a professional marketer who keeps abreast of what is happening in direct mail and, most importantly, in the list market. A broker, as the name implies, serves two sides. On the one hand, the broker is responsible to the list owner who pays the broker's commission (usually 20 percent of the basic list rental price). On the other hand, the broker has the responsibility of serving the needs of the mailer by recommending lists that are appropriate for the particular product or service the mailer wants to promote. This is a tightrope which the conscientious, responsible list brokers have learned to walk with intelligence and integrity.

Any professional list broker can furnish upward of 95 percent of all

the available lists. While some mailers work with many brokers, most prefer as a matter of control and efficiency to use one or two (at most, three) brokers. By limiting the number of brokers to be consulted, the mailer benefits by establishing a closer professional relationship with those selected.

A professional relationship will not work if the list broker operates in a vacuum. The mailer must view the broker as part of the total marketing process. To be most effective, the broker must have an interactive relationship with the individuals charged with the marketing, creative, financial, and analytical responsibilities for direct mail promotions.

The list professional can lend invaluable assistance in researching the list market to determine whether a definable market for the product or service exists or must be reached by inference or affinity relationship. This research provides a valuable tool for the creative side of the mailer's business. Experienced creative professionals agree that writing copy without an understanding of the market the way it exists (and not the way one hopes it exists) is laboring blind. The less they know about the market, the less directed the copy and the less likely that it will be successful. As members of your marketing team, these practitioners will go beyond the list recommendations. They will suggest testing patterns, comment on promotional packages, and assist in analyzing and interpreting response.

The advantages in establishing a relationship with a broker are specific and definable. The list professional has:

1. Information on and access to all the lists available and knows how individual lists can be clustered to represent a market
2. Knowledge of the responsiveness of individual lists for various services and products sold by mail
3. The ability to submit specific, pinpointed recommendations based on experience with similar products and services
4. The experience to assist in designing the list test matrix

In addition, and very important, the list broker will handle the considerable details involved in list rental transactions.

To establish an effective business relationship with a list broker:

1. Bring the broker into the picture at an early stage to help profits and to help in the approach to the market.
2. Take the broker into your confidence. Trade secrets will be respected.
3. Give the broker *time* to do a skillful job since she or he must make specific recommendations and supply information such as balance counts, selectivity, and state counts.
4. Define the relationship to be established with a broker. If you prefer working with many brokers, the list decisions will be yours to make.

This system can work, but most mailers do not have the necessary knowledge to make the proper list selections.

In the list brokerage field a broker is measured by the success factor in list recommendations, just as stock brokers are measured by the success factor of stocks recommended for purchase. (List brokers do better!)

LIST COMPILERS

There are two types of *compilers*: those who specialize in the business and professional markets and those who compile lists in the consumer market. (Some companies do both.) Compiling a list is an intricate process. In most instances, to make a list effective as a market requires experience in developing sources for the names and developing the methodology for producing lists with a high degree of accuracy.

The compiled business and professional lists are derived from a variety of printed sources: telephone directories, classified telephone directories (yellow pages), business and industrial directories, professional and association membership rosters, and government and state information. In the United States, there is a *Directory of Directories* that contains over 5200 entries and covers a broad variety of disciplines and markets.

The consumer list compilers use sources such as census information, auto registrations, surveys, questionnaires, and telephone directories. These compilations can be selected on a variety of criteria: head of household by name, median income by geographic area, age of head of household, occupation, single-family dwelling unit, and other demographic factors.

To give you an idea of the scope of consumer compilations, here is a quote from a prospectus about Metromail, one of the pioneers in this field:

> Metromail has a data base with marketing-oriented information on 150 million individuals and 76 million of a total 85 million American households. President William Howe has headed operations since 1969, when it belonged to Metromedia. The company went public in April 1984.
>
> Metromail's fastest-growing business is developing and enhancing mailing lists. Names, addresses and telephone numbers are taken directly from telephone directories, then supplemented by census, driver's license and other data to tell customers exactly how old, rich, educated, free-spending and so on we are. Metromail also does a big business in mail production, sending one billion pieces annually for customers such as Reader's Digest. Its Cole Publications unit prints "reverse phone books," with listings arranged by address and telephone number, which are the bibles of newspaper newsrooms and police stations.

In general, compiled lists offer the opportunity to saturate a particular market segment. The list compiler, therefore, is an integral part of the interactive discipline.

LIST MANAGERS

List managers perform a media function for the list owner. Most list owners are involved in a basic business and do not wish to allocate internal human and financial resources to the business of renting their lists. This is where the list manager comes in. Please bear in mind, however, that some companies do have in-house list managers (Columbia House, Ziff-Davis, Hanover House, American Express, to mention just a few).

In the *DMA Fact Book on Direct Marketing,* the definition of a list manager is as follows:

> One who, as an employee of a list owner or as an outside agent, is responsible for the use, by others, of a specific mailing list(s). The list manager serves the list owner in several or all of the following capacities: list maintenance (or advice thereon), list promotion and marketing, list clearance and record keeping, collecting for use of the list by others.

The objective of list management is to maximize list rental income. In order to do this, list managers must have the capability to develop creative advertising promotions, must understand the dynamics of direct mail, and must respond to fiduciary responsibilities. Meeting fiduciary responsibilities requires monthly financial reports, consistent collection procedures, and prompt remittances to the list owner.

List managers work mostly through list brokers. List managers are judged by the sophistication of their list marketing strategies and the generation of list rental income for the list owner.

SERVICE BUREAUS

The advent of Zip codes in 1967 propelled the list community into the computer age. List owners quickly found that to add Zip codes to a list was accomplished more accurately and more quickly by computerizing the list and then matching it against a table of Zip codes. This brought the list maintenance service bureau into a prominent role in our business.

Today, the service bureaus have expanded into sophisticated facets of data processing and data conversion activities beyond file maintenance. One of the most recognized of these functions is duplication elimination, popularly known as "merge/purge." Again, it was the introduction of Zip codes which made it possible to develop the system to examine names and addresses and omit duplicates. There are different programs developed by service bureaus for this elimination process. The most common method is the use of a "match code" whereby the computer looks at the Zip code and small portions of the name and address. Other systems use the Zip code but compare full name and address, which provides a more accurate match. Any system that helps to eliminate more duplicates is bound to be cost-effective. But some systems do "overkill," and that is not response effective.

Complete reports which are necessary for accounting purposes are generated for the mailer. Some of these are:

Input control. To verify quantity, any exclusion criteria requested by the user, and deliverability of name and address

Duplicate identification report. Shows quantity and percent of duplication for each list against all the lists included in the mailing

Net names by mail key. Shows the number of names from each list in key number sequence

Other services performed are: computer letters, Zip coding, name suppression (DMA preference file, Zip codes, states, bad pay, etc.), extracting statistically valid cells required for test purposes, statistical reports, generation of labels properly keyed, carrier route and five-digit Zip code presorting, and delivering the output to the letter shop in the most cost-effective manner for the mailer.

LETTER SHOPS

The direct mail process stops at the letter shop because it's the last link in the chain that begins with a concept and ends in the mail. The following is a research report released by The Kleid Company about 2 decades ago.

THE LETTER SHOP: LAST LINK IN THE CHAIN

Delays seem inevitable in the production of direct mail. It's the exception when artists, writers, printers, envelope manufacturers or list houses are not fighting deadlines. Delays compound, time slips away but everyone hopes that the letter shop, the last link in the chain, will make up the lost time. But the mailing houses have many accounts who mail in volume during the peak period with the result that overtime charges pile up and mail dates slip away.

Here's how to work with your mailing house:
1. Discuss plans in advance. Let your shop specify the requirements for automatic inserting and labeling. Ask how they want material packed and delivered (open skids, small bundles, or cartons). Schedule mail dates to

assure continuous daily production. Give the shop lead time to coordinate your work with mailings for other accounts.

2. Do not allow the printer to mix different weight paper stock on the same job. This causes problems when the mail is weighed in at the post office for third-class handling.

3. Make sure that the envelope house designs the envelopes for automatic inserting. Cellophane should be properly affixed over windows, and flaps should not stick together.

4. Sorting third-class mail is difficult. Allocate sufficient time so that the letter shop can do the job properly.

5. Make sure that all components of a shipment are clearly marked or labeled. With the mountains of material moving in and out of any big shop, something is bound to go astray.

6. Don't ask your letter shop to advance postage money or express charges. Letter shop work is mostly labor. With competitive prices, there's no room for banking services.

7. Don't ask the shop to store odds and ends and overruns. This is an expense which is never figured in estimating. It is costly to hold material for a year or two without compensation.

8. Request a daily written report indicating receipt of materials, postage, and express charges plus daily and cumulative mailing counts by keys.

Most of these basics still apply, but with the implementation of the three-tier rate structure for first-, second-, and third-class mail, there are new requirements in the preparation of mail. Mailers must be familiar with the new rules in order to take full cost benefits offered by presorting into carrier, five-digit Zip codes, and the balance which can't be sorted into either. Letter shops, of necessity, are fully aware of the regulations. Based on the total quantity of the mailing, they can give advice on exactly how the names and addresses should be delivered to them in order to maximize cost savings.

CREATIVITY: THE COHESIVE FABRIC

Traditionally, it seemed to be standard operating procedure for a mailer to set up the offer and promotional literature and then seek the audience. Logically it makes better sense to define the potential market first and tailor the promotion accordingly. And it's not all demographics which traditionally involve a raw data profile of the typical citizen of a community. Demographics may no longer serve as the best means of selecting the optimum target market nor as the best means of focusing the copy.

If we keep in mind that consumer attitudes, values, and lifestyles are changing, then we must be more concerned with attitudes and preferences which dictate what the consumer will spend and for what. This is *psychographic detailing*. And marketing in the future will require evaluation and access on this basis.

Case in point: In a program developed to study affinity patterns, it was ascertained that the people who subscribe to *House & Garden* are prime prospects not only for expensive offers but for quality appeals: articles, ideas, and activities for people with a special flair, taste, and style. You can sell anything from a clearly functional $10 kitchen utensil to a $450 collection of esoteric recordings, a book of poems, a bolt of hand-loomed fabric, or the worthiness of a particular charity.

On the other side of the coin, copy that is too focused limits the universe, for example, an outdoor magazine (not hunting and fishing) with a backpacker, outward-bound editorial theme plus some sprinkling of conservation. If the copy is directed to an upscale audience similar to the Sierra Club, you will be writing to a limited audience. In this instance, if the list market were expanded to include outdoor enthusiasts in general, nature lovers, buyers of books about the animal kingdom, and contributors to animal causes, you could look at the sources from which these names were acquired and then broaden the copy focus to embrace the entire logical market, not just one specific, limited segment.

Another situation: a self-help magazine for women. The mailing package looked like an upscale fashion offer rather than a behavioral self-improvement offer. Not only did it convey fashion but the lady on the package was happy, young, and pretty. There was no indication that she wasn't "in command." The brochure was the same, with happy and family-oriented scenes. This image was not an accurate one for the magazine since editorial was keyed specifically to self-understanding and coping with family problems. The copy did not accurately portray the magazine, nor did it allow the development of a responsive list market. Actually, the prototype of the magazine indicated that the prospects were on the lower end of the economic and educational scale and would more likely be the type of people who would write to the behavioral advice columnists in local newspapers. Had the list market been defined first, the copy would have been so directed, and the first direct mail effort would not have bombed the way it did.

In the prospect's mind, the product or service represents a host of both tangible and intangible attributes, which means that you must sell the benefits. The relationship between product and copy is clear, as should be the synergism between copy and list. A successful direct mail campaign takes creativity on every front. Copy language has an infinite number of possibilities. Lists have a "flavor." You're juggling important forces into the promotional effort.

CONCLUSION

While it is necessary to point out the competitive nature among the companies within each of these disciplines, there is the moment of truth when each company is working for a mutual client. It is then essential to provide the cooperation necessary to achieve a responsive and cost-effective mailing program for the mutual client—the mailer.

Caveat: The coordination of all the various suppliers and creative resources requires a high degree of sophistication and professionalism. Companies should not attempt to undertake this function with people who are not completely familiar with all the aspects of direct mail marketing. If there is no one within the company who has this expertise, the company should use a consultant or direct marketing agency. Increasingly, major corporations are entering the direct marketing field, where there have been absolute disasters because of the inapplicability of general marketing principles to the direct marketing discipline.

CHAPTER 3

What Is Meant by "Renting" Lists?

William Shakespeare appears to have been concerned about lists, judging from *Henry IV, Part I* (Act I, Scene 2): "I would to God thou and I knew where a commodity of good names were to be bought."

Shakespeare should have said "rent" instead of "bought" because 99 percent of all list transactions are on a *one-time* rental basis. Lists can be purchased outright, but that requires special negotiations and certain conditions. It is not normally done.

Renting lists usually involves certain important conditions:

1. The names are rented for *one-time use* only. No copy of the list may be retained for any purpose whatsoever. The only names that can be retained are those of customers or potential customers who respond to your offer.
2. The rental of a list must be cleared with the list owner in advance, and a sample of the mailing piece must be submitted. The list owner has the right of approval or disapproval. The mailing piece approved is the only one that can be used.
3. No reference to the list being used can appear in the promotional package because this might be construed by the recipient as an endorsement of the product or service being offered.

4. The mailing date approved by the list owner must be adhered to. If the approved date cannot be met, a new mail date must be cleared.
5. List owners have a basic rental charge (typically $40 to $60 to $100 for each 1000 names). Most list owners charge extra for selecting names on the basis of gender, recency, Zip code, location, unit of sale, or some other segmentation available in the particular list. There are no standard rates. Pricing is dependent on the quality of the list. All charges are on a per thousand name basis. Incidentally, no one seems to know how the 1000 (M) quantity evolved as the measuring unit in direct mail, but it certainly does simplify the arithmetic.

WHY WOULD YOU RENT YOUR INTERNAL LISTS?

Most companies rent their lists primarily because of the revenue to be gained. Net revenue ranges from a few thousand dollars to $3 million or more annually. *Example:* Assume a list of 500,000 names rents at $50 per thousand (less 20 percent commission). The list turns over 10 times in a year—5,000,000 at $40 per thousand equals $200,000. When approximately 10 percent is added for selection charges, the total becomes $220,000. If it costs about $3 to run the names, the net profit is $205,000. Most of this income goes down to the bottom line. It would be interesting to do a projection on how much business you would have to transact to net that kind of profit.

Another benefit is a form of market research. Many companies are able to improve their own selection of rental lists by monitoring the successful outside usage of their house file. For example, a catalog company uses the *Architectural Digest* list successfully. *Architectural Digest* would certainly test the customer list of the particular catalog company. A food catalog finds the *Food & Wine* and *Bon Appetit* subscriber file responsive. It makes sense for *Food & Wine* and *Bon Appetit* to try the food company's customer file.

WHAT PRICE SHOULD YOU CHARGE?

The pricing of a list for rental purposes requires a good deal of thought, and the same kind of research that is required for the pricing of any product. One of the first steps is to consult with a list broker or manager to get a feel for the pricing on lists similar to yours. If the list represents an interest-defined market such as sophisticated, affluent investors, a relatively higher price can be sustained.

Generally speaking and based on experience, however, most mailers react negatively to a list that rents at $100 or over. At this point a financial projection, with input from a list broker or manager, should be structured. Assuming a list of 100,000 names and the projected number of turnovers based on the price sensitivity factor, let's look at what happens at different price levels:

Per M	Projected Turnovers	Projected Quantity	Net Income
$125	15	1,500,000	$150,000
100	20	2,000,000	160,000
80	30	3,000,000	192,000

The difference from high to low is $42,000. If the objective of list rental income is maximizing profit, then pricing must be quantified. In some instances, for example, list owners who use their house list successfully and frequently to cross-promote internal products, the pricing aspect is used to curtail outside list rental activity. This type of thinking is open to question.

In any case, it is important that you review your objectives carefully and evaluate this aspect of your business as an income stream leading right down to the bottom line.

HOW DO YOU PROTECT YOUR LIST FROM BEING COPIED?

"Seed" or "decoy" names added to your list will reveal most unauthorized use. These decoys should be distinctive and easily recognized. Your name is John J. Harper and your address is 305 East Hartsdale Avenue, Hartsdale, New York 10530. The variations can come out as John A. Harper, John B. Harper, John C. Harper, and so on except for using the initial J. Or you could change Harper to Halper, Haper, or Harder. As long as you document the usage accurately, unauthorized use can be detected. *One warning:* Do not respond to any solicitation under the seed or decoy. This does happen and creates problems. In addition, mailers guarantee as a condition of the rental agreement, that the names will be used only once and that no copy will be retained in any shape, manner, or form. (See Chapter 14 for further details.)

HOW MANY TIMES CAN A LIST BE RENTED?

Lists can be rented as often as once a week. The companies which rent your names may reorder the same names two or three times a year. Hence, if your list is well-maintained, it is a continuing source of income year after year.

IN WHAT QUANTITIES WILL YOUR NAMES BE ORDERED?

Tests will run from 5000 to 10,000 or more, depending upon the requirements of the mailer. If results are satisfactory, you will receive reorders for more sizable quantities or for the balance of the list.

HOW LARGE MUST A LIST BE TO CREATE INTEREST?

The usual minimum is 25,000 recent names. The minimum can be smaller, however, on lists representing a specific field of interest.

WHAT IS THE PAYMENT PROCEDURE?

After you have completed and shipped the order, you submit a bill to the broker. As your agent, the broker will invoice the mailer. Upon receipt of payment, the broker will remit payment less the usual 20 percent commission.

IS IT NECESSARY TO SIGN A CONTRACT WITH THE BROKER TO HANDLE YOUR LIST?

No written contract or agreement is necessary. You are under no obligation to accept orders. You may withdraw your list at any time with appropriate notice to the users who have tested your list. The only possible exception to the necessity for a contract would occur should your list be represented by a list manager.

HOW IS LIST INFORMATION SUPPLIED?

If you decide to offer your list for rental through a broker or list manager, the broker or manager will provide what is known in the trade as a *data card,* prepared based on details received from you, the list owner. The cards are designed to present complete, accurate information that will permit the broker and the client to select the list that best fits the marketing situation at hand. Chart 3.1 illustrates a typical data card and identifies the key types of information provided.

Chart 3.1 *Changing Times: Kiplinger Magazine for Money Management* **Data Card**

1. 1,040,647 subscribers @ $55/M *Can Select:*	*Minimum: 5000*
2. Monthly hotline (quantity varies) @ $60/M Monthly address changes (avg. 5000) @ $60/M 600,000 long-term subscribers (2 years or more)@ $60/M	
3. For magtape, add $20 per reel for nonreturnable tape.	
4. **Data** A monthly magazine of family money management ideas. Includes: ideas to avoid excess spending in taxes, insurance, real estate, buying a car and appliances; inflation safeguards; tips on health, vacations, gardening. 97% at home address.	*Sample required* on all tests *and* continuations.
5. **Unit** $15 per year; introductory subscription $8 per year.	
6. **Media** Direct mail, space, radio, TV, agents.	Allow 3 weeks for addressing after sample is approved.
7. **Profile** 73% married; 73% own home, co-op, or condominium; 55% between ages 25 and 54; 33% professional/technical/managerial; 51% attended and/ or graduated college (27% have done postgraduate work); 57% have household income of $25,000+.	
8. **Filed** Zip sequence; 4-up Cheshire or magtape (9T/1600). DMMA Mail Preference Service used.	
9. **Sex** 57% men. Can select 496,883 identifiable men @ N/C. See card 17190 for Selection for Women's titles.	Net name arrangement: (50,000 minimum) 85% + $5.00/M (must be reciprocal).

10. **Select** *N*th name @ N/C.
 State/SCF/Zip @ $3.50/M (can use Zip tape).
 Pressure-sensitive labels @ $3.25/M.
 Split test @ $3.50/M.
 Business address @ $3.50/M.
 Individual name and title select @ $3.50/M.
 Source @ $3.50/M:
   341,602 direct mail
   177,165 radio and TV
   399,830 agents (mostly direct response)
     2,442 space
     8,928 dept. stores
   91,803 miscellaneous	

11. **Keying** @ N/C.	

LIST EXCHANGES: AN EXTENSION OF LIST RENTALS

Quid pro quo (Something for something).

It can be highly profitable to exchange names with either competitive or noncompetitive companies if the markets are essentially the same or have an inferred affinity.

Equity is the important factor in each instance. Each side must offer names of comparable quality. However, if one company is offering expires for actives, a two-for-one or three-for-one exchange basis can be arranged. This rarely happens because each party usually requires a one-for-one exchange based on preestablished selection criteria.

There are substantial reasons why exchanges make sense:

1. Each side gains access to a list that might otherwise not be available to them.
2. Each side is using names of comparable quality, clean and active.
3. The savings of $50 to $70 per thousand in list rental charges (as opposed to a broker exchange rate of $5 to $8 per thousand) is often in itself sufficient to make exchanges profitable.

Let's take an example. List A rents at $60 per thousand, plus $6 per thousand for selection and an overall (excluding list) cost, in the mail of $200.

	Costs	Quantity	Total Cost	1% Response	CPO
Rental	$266	100,000	$26,600	1000	$26.60
Exchange	$206*	100,000	20,600	1000	$20.60

*Exchange rate at $6/M.

The variance in overall cost on 100,000 names favors the exchange by $6000 (22.6 percent). On a cost-per-order basis, the figures show $6 per order less (22.6 percent).

The financial implications are important to quantify. In the example stated, let's assume a maximum allowable order cost of $22. If we start from the premise that only profitable rental lists will be used in any direct mail campaign, the list in our example would not have been included on a rental basis. Yet, you must also consider the 1000 new customers. If the "customer value" is, let's say, $50, you could be losing $50,000 in potential sales.

If you compare these calculations against the loss of list rental income (100,000 × $60/M − 20 percent commission = $4800), the financial implications are quite clear.

The caveat with exchanges is to play the what-if game. If the exchange is *not* included, how will it affect your profit objectives? The resulting arithmetic will provide the decision-making information.

TOOLS OF THE TRADE

There are several procedural instruments which are used by list brokers and managers. Each company, obviously, designs its own forms.

Instrument	Application
Data card (Chart 3.1)	This information card is used to disseminate accurate, complete, and timely list information.
Request for up-to-date information	List information on the data card must be updated frequently. In order to remind the list owner to supply the information a communication is sent to him or her. These updated details guide the broker in deciding whether or not to recommend a particular list.
Clearance form	As mentioned earlier, it is standard procedure that the list owner be contacted in advance of placing the order for clearance and approval of the mailing piece and mail date. It is the list owner's prerogative to accept or reject usage.

EXPLANATORY NOTES FOR CHARTS 3.1 TO 3.4

Note that the following item numbers correspond to the line numbers in Chart 3.1.

1. Number of names available and description.
2. These are the special selections available. *Hotline* refers to recency. *Changes of address* represents subscribers who have moved within the last month. *Long-term subscribers* represents those people who have subscribed to this publication for 2 years or more.
3. If names are furnished on *magnetic tape*, which is a computer storage device for recording and reproducing defined information, payment for the tape is required.
4. Description of the editorial focus of the magazine.

5. Cost to the subscriber.
6. Sources used to acquire names.
7. Demographic information.
8. This indicates that the subscriber file is maintained in Zip code sequence and names will be furnished in this sequence to the user. The list can be supplied to the user on 4-up Cheshire labels or on magnetic tape. The "9 Track/1600 BPI" refers to the format of the magnetic tape which will be supplied. (*Track* refers to the storage channel, and *bits per inch* refers to the packing density.)
9. Sex selection. N/C means "no charge."
10. Other available selections and options. The "*N*th" refers to the methodology used by the list owner to extract a test sample across the entire file. The abbreviation SCF stands for *sectional center facility* and refers to the first three digits of the Zip code. Reference to "Zip tape" means that if the user has developed a tape of Zip codes which she or he wants omitted or selected, the list owner has the computer program which will enable the use of the tape to process the order. *Pressure-sensitive label* is a type of label with a gummed back enabling the recipient to remove the label and affix it to the order device. *Split test* refers to the capability of extracting two or more test cells on a comparable basis if the user is conducting a price, package, or copy test.
11. In a direct mail campaign each list much be assigned a key number in order to track response. This key number must be on the order form or response vehicle which goes back to the mailer. If the list is ordered on any type of label, the list owner is advising that they can imprint the key number at no extra charge.

When a mailer places a list rental order with a list broker, it is necessary that the order details be submitted to the list owner and/or service bureau. The list rental order supplies the specific instructions required for proper fulfillment of the order. Chart 3.2 covers lists ordered on magnetic tape. Chart 3.3 covers lists which are ordered on labels.

Instructions are pretty consistent except that label orders may require key number imprint. Magnetic tape orders have tape and net-name specifications, a request for tape layout and/or sample dump, and instructions on returning the magnetic tape to the list owner.

Shipping and identification labels (Chart 3.4) are supplied by the list broker or manager to ensure delivery of the list to the correct destination and to enable the service bureau or letter shop to identify the list properly.

Chart 3.2 Purchase Order for Cheshire Labels

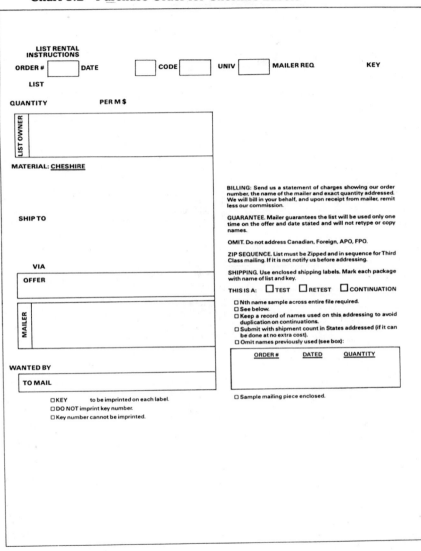

LIST RENTAL INSTRUCTIONS

ORDER # [　] DATE [　] CODE [　] UNIV [　] MAILER REQ　　KEY

LIST

QUANTITY　　　PER M $

LIST OWNER

MATERIAL: <u>CHESHIRE</u>

SHIP TO

VIA

OFFER

MAILER

WANTED BY

TO MAIL

☐ KEY　　to be imprinted on each label.
☐ DO NOT imprint key number.
☐ Key number cannot be imprinted.

BILLING: Send us a statement of charges showing our order number, the name of the mailer and exact quantity addressed. We will bill in your behalf, and upon receipt from mailer, remit less our commission.

GUARANTEE. Mailer guarantees the list will be used only one time on the offer and date stated and will not retype or copy names.

OMIT. Do not address Canadian, Foreign, APO, FPO.

ZIP SEQUENCE. List must be Zipped and in sequence for Third Class mailing. If it is not notify us before addressing.

SHIPPING. Use enclosed shipping labels. Mark each package with name of list and key.

THIS IS A: ☐ TEST　☐ RETEST　☐ CONTINUATION

☐ Nth name sample across entire file required.
☐ See below.
☐ Keep a record of names used on this addressing to avoid duplication on continuations.
☐ Submit with shipment count in States addressed (if it can be done at no extra cost).
☐ Omit names previously used (see box):

ORDER #	DATED	QUANTITY

☐ Sample mailing piece enclosed.

27

Chart 3.3   Purchase Order for Magnetic Tape

**LIST RENTAL
INSTRUCTIONS**

ORDER # [   ] DATE   [   ]   CODE [   ] UNIV [   ] MAILER REQ   KEY

LIST

QUANTITY   PER M $

LIST OWNER

MAGNETIC TAPE

BILLING: Send us a statement of charges showing our order number, the name of the mailer and exact quantity addressed. We will bill in your behalf, and upon receipt from mailer, remit less our commission.

SHIP TO

GUARANTEE. Mailer guarantees the list will be used only one time on the offer and date stated and will not retype or copy names.

OMIT. Do not address Canadian, Foreign, APO, FPO.

ZIP SEQUENCE. List must be Zipped and in sequence for Third Class mailing. If it is not notify us before addressing.

VIA

SHIPPING. Use enclosed shipping labels. Mark each package with name of list and key.

-OFFER

THIS IS A: ☐ TEST   ☐ RETEST   ☐ CONTINUATION

☐ Nth name sample across entire file required.
☐ See below.
☐ Keep a record of names used on this addressing to avoid duplication on continuations.
☐ Submit with shipment count in States addressed (if it can be done at no extra cost).
☐ Omit names previously used (see box):

MAILER

ORDER #	DATED	QUANTITY

WANTED BY

TO MAIL

☐ KEY   to be imprinted on each label.
☐ DO NOT imprint key number.
☐ Key number cannot be imprinted.

☐ Mailer will pay for gross quantity shipped.
☐ Mailer will pay for NET names mailed:

☐ MAILER: Shipping labels are enclosed for return of MAGNETIC TAPE by your computer bureau to:

Tape layout/sample dump. ☐ Include with shipment.
☐ Send immediately to:

☐ Sample mailing piece enclosed.

28

Chart 3.4   Shipping and Identification Labels

MAGNETIC TAPE ENCLOSED

Enclose one label inside package.
Use other as shipping label for outside of package.

> THE KLEID CO. (200 PARK AVENUE, NEW YORK, NY 10166)
> ARRANGED THE RENTAL OF THIS LIST

LIST

FROM

KLEID
ORDER #   REEL #

TO

SHIPPING AND IDENTIFICATION LABEL

Enclose one label inside package.
Use other as shipping label for outside of package.

> THE KLEID CO. (200 PARK AVENUE, NEW YORK, NY 10166)
> ARRANGED THE RENTAL OF THIS LIST

LIST

FOR

KEY   QUANTITY

TO

WRAP EACH KEY SEPARATELY ... IDENTIFY WITH PROPER LABEL

LIST

FOR

KEY   QUANTITY

THE KLEID COMPANY INC. • LIST BROKERS • 200 PARK AVE. NEW YORK, N.Y. 10017

APPENDIX 3A

The Direct Marketing Association's Guidelines for List Practices

I. GENERAL

All involved in the transfer, rental, sale or exchange of mailing lists—owners, managers, compilers, brokers and users, and their suppliers and agents—should follow these guidelines.

ARTICLE 1 ACCURACY IN DESCRIPTION OF LISTS

All concerned should fairly, objectively and accurately describe each list, particularly with respect to its content, age of names, selections offered, quantity, source and owner.

ARTICLE 2 ADVERTISING CLAIMS

Before and at the time of distributing a list data card or promoting or advertising a list as available for rental, those who promote the list should be prepared to substantiate any claims they make and should avoid any untrue, misleading, deceptive or fraudulent statements and any references that are disparaging of competitors or of those on the list.

ARTICLE 3 SCREENING OF OFFERS/LIST USAGE

All involved should establish and agree upon the exact nature of a list's intended usage prior to the transfer or permission to use the list. Samples of all intended mailings should be reviewed by all involved in the rental process, and only approved materials should be used in the mailing, and on an agreed upon date. Lists should not be transferred or used

Reprinted with permission from the Direct Marketing Association.

for an offer that is believed to be in violation of any of the DMA Guidelines for Ethical Business Practices.

ARTICLE 4 PROTECTION OF LISTS

All those involved with a list should be responsible for the protection of list data and should take appropriate measures to assure against unauthorized access, alteration or dissemination of list data. Those who have access to such data should agree in advance to use those data only in an authorized manner.

ARTICLE 5 ONE-TIME USAGE

Unless agreement to the contrary is first obtained from the list owner, a mailing list transaction permits the use of a list for one time only. Except for respondents to its own mailing, a list user and its agents may not transfer names or information to its own customer files or recontact names derived from a rented or exchanged list, or provide the names for another to make such contact, without prior authorization.

ARTICLE 6 DMA MAIL PREFERENCE
SERVICE/NAME REMOVAL OPTIONS

Every list owner who sells, exchanges, or rents lists should see to it that each individual on the list is informed of those practices, and should offer an option to have the individual's name deleted when rentals or purchases are made.

The list owner should remove names from its lists when requested directly by the individual, and by use of the DMA Mail Preference Service name removal list.

List brokers and managers should take reasonable steps to assure that list owners and compilers follow these list practices.

ARTICLE 7 PURPOSES OF
LISTS/LIST DATA

Lists should consist only of those data which are pertinent and necessary for marketing and related purposes. Direct marketers should transfer, rent, sell or exchange lists only for those purposes.

ARTICLE 8 LIST DATA/PRIVACY

All list owners, brokers, managers, compilers and users should be protective of the consumer's right to privacy and sensitive to the information collected on lists and subsequently considered for transfer, rental, sale or exchange. Information such as, but not limited to, medical, financial, insurance or court data and data that may be considered to be personal and intimate in nature by all reasonable standards should not be included on lists that are made available for transfer, rental, sale or exchange when there is a reasonable expectation by the consumer that the information would be kept confidential.

Any advertising or promotion for lists being offered for transfer, rental, sale or exchange should reflect a sensitivity for the individuals on those lists. Promotional methods and language that tend to portray characteristics of those individuals in a disparaging way should be avoided.

ARTICLE 9 LAWS, CODES, REGULATIONS AND GUIDELINES

Direct marketers should operate in accordance with all applicable laws, codes and regulations and with DMA's various guidelines as published from time to time.

Mailing list transactions are controlled by the legal principles affecting contracts. As such, mutual understanding, good faith, clear communication, defined terms and a meeting of the minds are imperative.

CHAPTER 4

Lists: The Smart Investment

The selection of mailing lists does not score high on the glamour index in direct mail; being creative is much more fun. But when response is analyzed, the list becomes *the bottom line* not only on its own responsiveness but relative to other tests conducted.

WHAT IS A MAILING LIST?

A mailing list consists of the names and addresses of a group of people or companies all having one or more things in common; the list represents a *meaningful grouping*.

Newcomers to direct mail will frequently talk about *a* list, one which they intend to compile themselves or find. However, it is rare that *one* list will do the job. You need to think in terms of markets.

By selecting the proper list, you can mail your offer to prospects who have demonstrated an interest in your kind of offer or who have the demographic and lifestyle characteristics which imply a high probability of interest. For example, to sell toys, you would select lists that tell you there is at least one child in the family. The prospects on the list could have bought juvenile items (books, records, magazines, clothing) or "parenting" products. The age of the child can be reasonably judged based on the item purchased. Lacking demonstrated evidence of children in the home, you might luck out once in every 15 to 20 list tests, but that's very expensive research.

LIST AVAILABILITY: POTENTIALS AND GUIDELINES

There are literally thousands of lists available covering every conceivable market you might be interested in reaching. Within each list, there are segments that you can select on the basis of geographic, demographic, behavioral, and other discriminants. This fragmentation increases the number of lists dramatically. So how do you determine, logically and practically, who or where your customers are?

There are two broad categories of lists: internal and external.

Internal. These lists are derived from a company's own files and typically represent units of customers, former customers, subscribers, former subscribers, donors, former donors, prospects, inquiries, employees, sales contacts, warranty cards, stockholders, and the like. For direct marketing companies, the customer list is an extremely valuable asset.

External. These lists fall into two categories; compiled and direct response.

COMPILATIONS

As mentioned previously, compiling lists is a business. There are many companies in the field whose only product line is lists. Basically there are two types of compilations: business and consumer. The business compiler uses trade directories, professional membership rosters, phone books, seminar registrants, and trade show exhibits.

Consumer or household compilers use census information, auto registrations, and surveys. These lists are extensively used for product sampling and couponing. However, the ability to segment by income, age, type of dwelling unit, occupation, number of children in the household plus other demographics suggests a variety of direct mail applications.

The world of compiled lists is vast: from "abattoirs" to "zoos"; from 100 names to 5 million; to household lists (such as Metromail, Polk, Donnelley) with a universe of 70 million-plus names representing most of the households in the United States.

While compiled lists provide no indication of which people have previously bought by mail, they do offer defined and identifiable markets. If your product appeals to a vertical (precisely defined) market such as doctors, dentists, lawyers, accountants, engineers, and educators, compiled lists offer the most complete coverage.

In the business field, compiled lists are widely available for major industry sections: agriculture, construction, manufacturing, transportation, communications, public utilities, wholesalers, retailers, finance, insurance, real estate, and service companies.

These business lists can be segmented on a variety of selectivity factors. One of the most widely used is the Standard Industrial Classification (SIC) system, which categorizes every type of commercial establishment, institution, and profession by assigning a specific four-digit number to each. They can also be segmented on the basis of financial strength, number of employees, geography, type of business organization (corporation, partnership, individual proprietorship), yellow page ad space, executive names by title, businesses which have just relocated, and so on. For example, Market Data Retrieval offers The American Executive Registry (Chart 4.1).

Chart 4.1 American Executive Registry, Individual Names

9,608,039	**Executives by Job Function**
3,150,289	**Executives by Company Size**
2,157,497	**Executives by Title** (chairperson of the board, board of directors, owner, co-owner, president, secretary, senior executive, group vice president, chief executive officer, vice president-planning, vice president-corporate development, senior corporate management, secretary and treasurer
6,095,057	**Executives by Industry** (agriculture, mining, construction, manufacturing non-durable, manufacturing durable, manufacturing metalworking, electronics /manufacturing, transportation, communications, utilities, wholesale durable, retail durable, retail nondurable, miscellaneous retail, banking, savings-loan-credit agency, insurance, real estate, personal services, business services, health, legal services, education, social service and organizations, miscellaneous services, government
171,718	**Data Processing Executives by Company Size**
187,207	**Data Processing Executives by Industry**
296,398	**Data Processing Executives by Title** (vice president-information systems, manager-systems and programming, manager-systems support, manager-data processing operations, manager-telecommunications, project manager, systems analyst, programmer-analyst, other data processing managers)

The registry is just one example of a business compilation. There are thousands more. These compilations are extensively used for business-to-business direct marketing which has been growing in direct proportion to the rising costs of personal sales calls and to the movement of companies into scattered locations throughout the country.

Direct mail, because of its measurability and accountability, affords the opportunity to target markets more precisely and to reach the decision makers. This is made possible by the ability through lists to test new markets and by developing a system to better qualify leads for direct mail or telephone selling. The follow-up sales method depends on the item(s) being offered. The key in a lead generation program is the *quality* of the lead. Too many unqualified leads, no matter how they are followed up, are wasteful of time and money.

The strategy here is to develop a business plan that realistically spells out the ratio of sales to leads required for profit based on allocation of financial and personnel resources, for example, a stock brokerage firm generating leads for account executives. Too many leads can be a disaster and have a negative effect if the participating office does not have sufficient, knowledgeable staff to handle the influx within a reasonable time frame and/or the leads must be turned over to a relatively inexperienced junior. This ingredient must be thoroughly addressed in the planning process. A mechanism must be set up that establishes the elements necessary for qualifying leads and also the conversion rate with a high degree of accuracy. This will make it possible to ascertain how many leads are required within a specified time frame and for each selling unit and could also point out the advisability of staggered mailings. In other words, to avoid the problem of too many leads at one time, lists could be ordered at one time but mailed weekly, biweekly, or on some other schedule.

In the *educational* market, you can reach the institutions by such factors as pupil enrollment, type of school, and grade level. Teachers within these schools can be grouped by grade and subject taught. At the college level, there are compiled lists of student names selectively organized on the basis of class, gender, field of study, tuition levels of the college or university, and a multitude of other choices.

The world of compiled lists is vast and complex because of the many options available. To judge a list on its quality as a mass will not be as profitable as selecting and testing it on a variety of identifiers. One approach to selectivity is to define what is perceived to be the prime audience relative to the needs that the product or service fulfills. In looking at such a matrix, you should not only be able to decide the initial market to tap but to expand directionally into other markets. Careful tracking on a consistent basis will identify marketing direction and action.

DIRECT RESPONSE LISTS

Although considered a type of external list, these are in fact the internal customer lists of other companies. These lists contain only the names of people who have already responded to a direct marketing effort (direct mail, space, radio, TV, telephone). Therefore, if you obtain access to such lists, you know you will be mailing to people with a demonstrated receptivity to buying by mail and/or any other direct marketing media. People who do *not* respond to these direct solicitations are *not* on direct response lists.

Direct response lists cover a broad scope of subjects of interest representing subscribers to magazines, newsletters, and books in the business, financial, hobby, health, sports, entertainment, religious, science, and cultural categories. Then you can reach people who have bought all types of merchandise: high fashion, sporting goods, gourmet foods, utilitarian items such as tools, and home improvement plans from thousands of catalogs and offers. Members of book and record clubs represent another specific market as do donors to charitable organizations.

The potential universe offered by direct response lists in the United States is almost 1 billion names, which is over 10 times the number of households and 5 times the total population (Chart 4.2). Staggering! Considering this vast universe of lists, the billions of pieces of promotion

Chart 4.2   Review of List Markets by Category

Category	Number of Lists	Universe (000)
Business and finance	1,207	166,026
New technology	163	9,478
Education, science, the professions	180	15,964
Fund raising	180	34,780
Hobbies and special interests	970	156,616
Entertainment	334	53,929
Reading	437	68,421
Self-improvement, health, religion	554	196,108
Women, home interest, family, general merchandise	769	255,353
Mixed media	254	66,441
Subtotal	4,794	956,675
Telephone marketing	97	71,361
Compiled	217	141,937
Canadian	350	97,119
Foreign	33	2,249
Total	5,745	1,335,782

Note: The duplication factor is not quantifiable, but it certainly does exist.

mail sent out each year, and the thousands of companies using direct mail, it would be an awesome task for any individual or company to keep afloat in the continuing stream of list information. But there is a solution: let the list consultant do the research. Examples of direct response lists follow.

Business and Finance

Kiplinger Washington Letter, Business Week, Fortune, Forbes, Boardroom Reports, California Business, Inc., Dow Theory, Financial World, Tax Angles, Savvy, Cashflow Magazine, Drawing Board, Baldwin-Cook, DayTimers, Changing Times, Money Magazine, Sylvia Porter's Personal Finance Magazine, Industry Week, Automotive News, Engineering and Mining Journal, Doan's Agricultural Report, Big Farmer, Progressive Farmer.

New Technology

Software News, Computer World, Infoworld, Insider, PC World, Compute.

Education, Science, the Professions

Arts and Activities, Learning Magazine, Education Digest, Drug Topics, Medical Arts Press, Science News, Physicians and Sports Medicine Magazine, American Journal of Nursing, Social Casework, American Psychological Association, Psychology Today.

Fund Raising

Common Cause, National Taxpayers Union, Disabled American Veterans, Animal Protection Institute, North Shore Animal League, Save the Redwoods League.

Hobbies and Special Interest

Better Homes and Gardens Crafts Club, Vogue Patterns Magazine, Needlecraft for Today Magazine, Ski Magazine, Boating, L. L. Bean, Golf Digest, Equus Magazine, Flying Magazine, Sports Illustrated, Yachting, Backpacker Magazine, Baseball Digest, Bass Fishing News, Snowmobile Magazine, Bowhunter Magazine, Car and Driver, Hot Rod, Motorcyclist Magazine, Popular Photography, Family Handyman, Brookstone, Jackson and Perkins, Horticulture Magazine, Organic Gardening, Colonial Homes, Collectibles Illustrated, Isaac Asimov's Science Fiction Magazines.

Entertainment, Lifestyle, Upscale

Architectural Digest, W Magazine, M Magazine, Stereo Review, Ovation Magazine, Columbia House, Wisconsin Cheeseman, Food and Wine, Bon Appetit, Sixty Minute Gourmet, Travel and Leisure, Touring and Travel, Cruise Travel Magazine, Island Magazine, New York Dance Foundation, Live from Lincoln Center, Little Orchestra Society, New York Philharmonic, Chess Life, Popular Bridge, Games, Playboy, Esquire.

Reading (General and Cultural)

Time-Life Books, Saturday Review, Atlantic, Art News, American Artist Magazine, Discover, Geo, Archaeology, Harper's, American History Illustrated, New Republic, World Press Review, Doubleday Books, Time, Mother Earth News, People, Conservative Digest, U.S. News and World Report, Europe Magazine, Washington Post Weekly, Newsweek, Southern Living, Texas Monthly, Washingtonian, New York Magazine, Philadelphia Magazine, Ellery Queen, Boston Magazine, Life.

Self-Improvement, Health, Religion

Income Opportunities, Success Unlimited, Money Making Opportunities, Sweepstakes Magazine, Home Business News, Prevention Magazine, Weight Watchers Magazine, Nutrition Health Review, Harvard Medical School Health Newsletter, Fit Magazine, American Health Magazine, Catholic Digest, Christian Herald, Biblical Archaeology Review.

Home Interest, Families, Merchandise, Fashion

Lillian Vernon, Mark Cross, Horchow, Ambassador Leather Goods, Spiegel's, Hanover House, Spencer Gifts, Child Life, Xerox Summer Weekly Reader, Parents' Magazine, Cricket, Grolier, Gifted Children's Newsletter, Family Journal, Muppet Magazine, Teenage Magazine, Family Learning Magazine, McCall's Working Mother.

CLASSIFYING LISTS

This proliferation of lists pointed to the problem involved in selecting appropriate lists from such a large pool of availability. The probability of selecting new lists successfully was becoming more difficult at the same time that direct mail was becoming more expensive. The answer came from the computer and mathematicians. The objective was to create an electronic data base system that would provide quick and comprehensive access to list marketing information.

Utilizing the ability of the computer to process large-scale data banks, the first step was to go back to previous manual records for a period of 4 years. The next step was to categorize all the products sold into 50 product groups. For each product group, the data base contains the lists used for that particular group, for example, every list used to promote financial publications, news magazines, nature series, or home interest.

Since the thrust of the project was to develop a specialized procedure that would improve the probability of selecting test lists that would be successful for a given product, it appeared this could be achieved by a better understanding of the behavior of *groups* of consumers. For added value, the file was re-sorted by list, and the product groups were re-sorted using each list.

Chart 4.3 shows activity on list 1 for the year 1984. The total universe of this list is 1 million names. The total usage of 26 million names indicates that the list was turned over 26 times in 1 year, which points out the effectiveness of this list. It also reflects $1,300,000 in list rental revenue to the list owner at a net price including selections of approximately $50 per thousand.

Chart 4.3   Data Card Activity By Product Group, Calendar Year, List 1

Product Group	Total		Percent of Total Orders	Percent of Total Quantity
	Quantity (000)	Orders	Retests and Continuations	
Business and financial	11,768	88	33.1	45.3
Cultural reading	1,349	22	8.3	5.2
Entertainment	100	1	0.4	0.4
Educational, technical, professional	20	1	0.4	
Fund raising	2,810	49	18.4	10.8
Home interest	645	13	4.9	2.5
Hobbies and related subjects	1,435	21	7.9	5.5
News magazines	4,065	32	12.0	15.7
Regional magazines	428	21	7.9	1.7
Self-improvement	3,343	18	6.7	12.9
	25,963	266		

Note: Separate records are kept for tests. Tests are not always followed up quickly, and a test without a continuation would suggest failure, based on the evaluation process.

Chart 4.4 represents a list very similar to list 1, with a universe of 600,000 names. This list turned over 30 times. It is interesting to note that the same product groups were successful:

	List 1	List 2
Business and financial	45.3	52.4
News magazines	15.7	13.6
Self-improvement	12.9	11.5
Fund raising	10.8	5.8
Hobbies and related subjects	5.5	7.5
Cultural reading	5.2	3.9
Home interest	2.5	2.0
Regional magazines	1.7	1.7
Entertainment	0.4	1.6
Educational, technical, professional	—	—

Chart 4.4   Data Card Activity By Product, Calendar Year, List 2

	Retests and Continuations			
	Total		Percent of Total Orders	Percent of Total Quantity
Product Group	Quantity (000)	Orders		
Business and financial	9,618	186	55.4	52.4
Cultural reading	709	17	5.0	3.9
Entertainment	290	6	1.8	1.6
Fund raising	1,071	28	8.3	5.8
Home interest	334	9	2.7	2.0
Hobbies and related subjects	1,381	18	5.4	7.5
News magazines	2,540	36	10.7	13.6
Regional magazines	306	19	5.7	1.7
Self-improvement	2,103	17	5.0	11.5
	18,352	336		

In looking at this analysis, a guide emerges. These two lists can be recommended with a high confidence index for products and services in the first three categories and very selectively within the fund raising category. Regional magazines can be considered because the low percentage is influenced by the quantity available in the geographic market served by these publications. Based on this analysis, the other product categories should not test these lists. However, this is not necessarily true.

Depending on the level of the retest response (and the product or service being offered), subsequent studies showed that certain portions of these lists could be used, for example, selection by gender, geographics, and source.

This clustering and labeling points to a dimension of consumer behavior which can be utilized in future selection of lists for the promotion of any given product. There are underlying factors in each cluster which show an affinity for certain kinds of products. Affinity marketing forms the basis for suggesting and testing lists of prospects who have, by an associative action, revealed an interest in a certain type of product or service.

THE GROWTH OF DATA BASES

In general terms almost any list can be considered a data base; many successful direct marketers consider their house list (internal customer file) one, and rightfully so, if we refer to the dictionary definition of "data base" as a collection of data organized for rapid search and retrieval (as by computer). See Charts 6.1 and 6.2 as examples of internal data bases.

At this time, in terms of common industry terminology, a *list data base* represents a merged group of lists with a unifying theme with duplication removed. The data base can be accessed based on a number of determinates (see Chart 6.2).

However, advanced research techniques and technologies have brought about an important new "databasing" trend which has evolved over the past several years and which is based on psychographics, that is, personal interests. Lifestyle Selector (Denver, Colorado) was a pioneer in this field. The methodology used was to enclose questionnaires with warranty card distribution for an extensive variety of products. (Lifestyle Selector did advise the recipient that the information on the questionnaire would be used as part of a mailing list. The recipients were offered the right to request that their names not be included on the list. Very important!)

The lifestyle characteristics which can be accessed are shown on Chart 4.5. Another important opportunity in testing this type of list is to establish affinity patterns. For example, through careful and structured testing by an upscale, high-ticket merchandise offer, it was found that art and antiques, collectibles, cultural and art objects, foreign travel, and photography represented a market affinity. The only other criteria superimposed in the testing stage was a selection based on income.

Chart 4.5   Lifestyle Selector

	Approximate Quantities		Approximate Quantities
Art and antique collecting	1,330,000	Hunting and/or shooting	1,974,000
Automotive work	1,512,000	Money making	96,000
Bible and/or devotional	338,000	opportunities	
reading		Motorcycling	1,144,000
Bicycling	2,667,000	Needlework and/or	2,890,000
Boating or sailing	1,912,000	knitting	
Book readers	2,355,000	Our nation's heritage	130,000
Bowling	665,000	Personal computer	324,000
CB radios	878,000	Photography	2,507,000
Cable TV viewing	827,000	Physical fitness and/or	2,836,000
Camping and/or hiking	2,960,000	exercise	
Collectibles	1,093,000	Racquetball	1,000,000
Community or civic activities	860,000	Real estate investment	700,000
Coupon users	2,389,000	Recreational vehicle	966,000
Crafts	2,278,000	(4-wheel drive)	
Cultural and arts events	1,244,000	Running or jogging	1,593,000
Electronics	766,000	Science and new	249,000
Fashion clothing	1,060,000	technology	
Fishing	3,251,000	Science fiction	523,000
Foreign travel	1,454,000	Self-improvement	700,000
Gardening and/or plants,	2,875,000	Sewing	2,863,000
homeowners		Skiing	1,447,000
Gardening and/or plants,	818,000	Stamps and/or coin	787,000
renters		collecting	
Golf	1,662,000	Stereo, records, and	3,988,000
Gourmet foods and cooking	1,816,000	tapes	
Grandchildren	148,000	Stock and bond	941,000
Health and natural foods	1,224,000	investment	
Home furnishing and	1,555,000	Sweepstakes entrants	2,164,000
decorating		Tennis	1,629,000
Home video games	1,475,000	Watching sports on TV	961,000
Home video recording	1,059,000	Wildlife and environ-	677,000
Home workshop	2,171,000	mental concerns	
Horse lovers	155,000	Wines	1,602,000
Household pets	1,193,000	Yuppies	465,000

ASK QUESTIONS

In direct mail you can control your package, your offer, and your product, but the rental *list*, so important to your success, is the one factor you can't really control. You don't own it, nor did you produce it. You are entirely dependent on outside parties for the accuracy of the information on which to base your decision.

It is *essential* to learn all there is to know about the lists you want to test. Ask for mailing pieces or samples of recent advertisements and find out where these ads appeared so that you can get a better idea of the "flavor" of the list.

Data cards you receive from brokers or list managers are necessarily truncated. There is usually a lot more to a list than what is shown on a data card, and the broker or manager can fill you in on how the list was put together and what kinds of mailers have been using it successfully.

Some list owners offer a heterogeneous mixture. Not satisfied with a small list of current buyers or subscribers, list owners will throw in expires, trials, and prospects just to fatten the universe. Ask the list broker or manager to ascertain whether or not the list owner will select by years or other criteria. If not, these types of lists should usually be avoided because old expires, former buyers, etc. almost never work. When they do work on a test, they almost invariably fall apart on the retest or continuation because, in the time lapse between test and continuation, the names didn't get fresher—they got older.

"Hotline" (recency) segmentation is very important and, in some cases, as important as the affinity factor. But be sure that the hotline is *hot*— not the last 12 months—and that the hotline represents a *paid* trans- action—not the name of someone who just received the premium, the free issue of a magazine, the free catalog, or the introductory record or book club offer or who was a "no" respondent to a sweepstakes offer. In summary, here are some list selection guidelines:

1. **Description** (subscribers, buyers, donors, expires, former buyers, etc.)
2. **Affinity** (based on the customer profile, previous list history, or a subjective extension of intuition or experience)
3. **Source used to acquire names** (direct mail, space, radio, TV, tele- phone)
4. **Recency**
5. **Frequency**
6. **Unit of sale**

However, if all lists that fail to qualify on all factors were to be eliminated, you might have no lists to test. It is essential to look at certain compensat- ing factors. If a list is particularly strong in its *affinity*, the other weaknesses may have to be overlooked. This is a correlation factor that needs to be addressed. For example, if a certain type of magazine does not qualify on the affinity factor, the paid hotline segment secured almost 100 percent by direct mail (source) within the preceding 30 days (recency) can prove to be responsive.

The final judgment can and should be carefully measured against the types of products and services which have used the list. But there is an extension to this. For example, list A has been used by a number of financial services. You can't empirically decide that you should test the list; what you must also consider is the type of financial product the list was used for. You're offering a sophisticated commodities futures product. List A was used by a broad scope of financial services, most of which, upon review, are found to be related to Keogh, IRA, cash management programs, etc. These services require a low financial commitment and suggest that capital safety is of prime importance. On the other hand, commodities, as an investment, are sophisticated. The rewards can be substantial, but there is a high element of risk. The prospects on list A have defined themselves as "nonriskers," and on those terms you would not test list A.

Cost Analysis: Managing the Numbers

It's a certainty that anyone using direct mail for the first time will immediately ask, "What response rate will I get?" or "What is an acceptable response rate?"

Response rate refers to the number of orders, donations, leads, and/or inquiries received for each 1000 pieces mailed. As mentioned previously, how the 1000 quantity (per M) evolved as the measuring unit in direct mail, no one seems to know. But it is definitely the accepted formula.

There is no standard or average response rate. Another company's response rate cannot be used as a basis for judgment or comparison. There are just too many variables that need to be considered. Essentially you should be looking at the level of response needed to accomplish your long-term business objectives rather than looking at response levels by themselves; doing so will help you maintain reasonable expectations. And, most important, the ultimate lifetime value of a customer must be factored into any equation used to establish how much you can afford to pay for a subscriber, buyer, member, donor, etc.

It is important, particularly in a start-up situation, to understand that in most instances the first mailing does not yield a profit. Actually, it should be considered a research and development (R&D) expense, which must be related to the stated goals of the business plan.

Even though you will get some orders which offset some of the expense, the most important result of the direct mail test is *information*. You will be able to determine the degree of acceptance of the product or service, and you will also learn which price, which promotional appeal, and which type of list work best. All in all, this method is much more directional than many other research methods.

HOW MUCH CAN YOU REALLY AFFORD TO PAY FOR AN ORDER?

Here are some basic guidelines: The fundamental calculation is the cost per order based on promotion (in the mail) costs. Just take the total promotion cost and divide it by the number of orders received. If your total promotion cost was $150,000 (500,000 pieces mailed at $300 per thousand), and you received a 1 percent response (5000 orders), your cost per order would be $30. In this example, if the product cost, fulfillment, returns, and bad debt were calculated at $20 and you were selling the product at $50, you'd know you were breaking even.

ALLOWABLE COST PER ORDER

Establishing how much you can afford to pay for an order is about the most pivotal figure in your statistical arsenal. The allowable cost per order (ACO) can and will vary. It won't even stay the same once you've established it because it is subject to change. For example, as volume goes up, do unit costs drop? What happens to the ACO if the price is raised? Many factors will force the allowable cost per order to fluctuate. But the important part is to find it first. Then you can alter it as the fundamentals change.

Let's take a look at the calculations involved in a book selling for $39.95 plus $1.25 for postage and handling (see Chart 5.1). If the cost per order is $17, the publisher breaks even on the sale. If the publisher spends less than $17, black ink shows on the bottom line.

While no one in business wants just to break even, profit goals begin with a break-even figure. The break-even analysis is a critical component of forecasting and is generally considered to be an excellent management decision-making tool. Breakeven is the point where there is no profit or loss. It is the point where costs exactly equal revenues. Because the breakeven is influenced by changes in fixed and variable expenses, it can illustrate the impact of different scenarios (the popular what-if approach). Obviously, the objective is not just to break even but to make a profit.

Chart 5.1 Allowable Cost Per Order (ACO)

Income

Selling price	$39.95
Postage and handling	1.25
Gross sale	$41.20
Returned books @ 25%	−10.30
Net Sales	$30.90

Expenses (Excluding Sales Expenses)

Manufacturing	$ 7.00
Returned books @ 25%	− 1.75
Net cost	$ 5.25

Then Add

Cartons, labeling, mailing	$ 1.07
Outgoing postage	0.94
Incoming postage	0.24
Refurbishing books	0.22
Bad debt (@ 10% of net sales)	3.09
Overhead (@ 10% of gross sales)	3.09
	$ 8.65
Total Cost	$13.90

Breakeven: Net sale $30.90 − total cost of $13.90 = $17.00.

However, understanding this balance point and the factors that can affect or change it is important in establishing goals and for evaluating assumptions. It is essential to remember that increased sales do not necessarily result in increased profits. For example, if the selling price is reduced, the breakeven may be forced up to a point at which a substantial increase in sales is required to break even. Break-even analysis is a problem-solving aid. It will not force a decision but will provide additional insights into how certain alternatives will affect the bottom line.

In the preceding example, as described in Chart 5.1, a goal of earning 10 percent profit to sales was set. What allowable order cost is required? To calculate, simply take 10 percent of your net sales and reduce your breakeven by that amount: $17.00 − $3.09 = $13.91; thus $13.91 is the allowable order cost to make 10 percent profit to sales (see Chart 5.2 for examples at various cost levels). The assumption here is that a more attractive mailing package will increase response. But even if this assump-

Chart 5.2   Examples at Various Cost Levels

Mailing Cost per Thousand	Quantity	Total Cost	Orders	Percent	CPO
$175	30,000	$5250	428	1.4	$12.27
200	30,000	6000	480	1.6	12.50
250	30,000	7500	510	1.7	14.70
300	30,000	9000	600	2.0	15.00

tion is accurate, the increase in response does not always compensate for the increase in costs.

The *allowable* is an important evaluation technique. It is a method to determine (list by list, space ad by space ad, all direct response media) whether or not you are meeting *profit* objectives. If you add the lifetime value of a customer to this equation, profits can then be estimated within a reasonable level. Think of ACO as a guide to be recalculated as conditions change. *Case in point*: let's look at a price increase. If you are able to raise your price without reducing the response, the profit will go up while the cost per order will remain the same. However, in most instances, a substantial increase in price will lower the response until the price sensitivity goes away.

Let's take another example which is much more complicated.

CONTINUITY PROGRAM

The product is a 20-volume encyclopedia, and volume 1 is offered free. Volumes 2 and 3 are shipped separately with a bill, on a 6-week cycle. If payment is received for either volume 2 or 3, the balance of the books (17 volumes) is shipped at once in bulk. The selling price for volumes 2 through 20 is $7.98 each, plus $1.25 for shipping and handling. The key element for profit and loss (P&L) statements is the acceptance factor on the bulk shipment. In most cases, 80 percent of the gross income is derived from the bulk shipment.

HOW TO CALCULATE THE DROP-OFF

This is how it all begins. If you can use hard historical information, life is easier. But if it's a *new* continuity program, estimates are necessary. Chart 5.3 shows both gross and net shipments calculated at each level, on the basis of 100 starters instead of a single one.

Chart 5.3 Continuity Program

1. Drop-off Percentages (Historical or Estimated)

	Percent
Vol. 1	100
Vol. 2	70
Vol. 3	50
Bulk shipment	25

2. Overall Number of Books

(1) Volume Number	(2) Gross Books Shipped	(3) Books Returned	(4) Net Books Shipped	(5) Single- Charge Books
Vol. 1 (free)	100	2.00 (2%)	98.00	
Vol. 2	70	14.00 (20%)	56.00	
Vol. 3	50	12.50 (25%)	37.50	93.50
Bulk (17 volumes)	425	63.75 (15%)	361.25	
Total charge books	545	90.25	454.75	
Single books	220	28.50	191.50	
Total books returned		92.25		

Explanation of terms: The *first column* is self-explanatory. The *second column* (Gross Books Shipped) is based on 100 starters. The *third column* (Books Returned) shows the number of books returned in relation to the volume number. And based on a 6-week cycle, column 3 gives you an estimated flow of returned books.

Column 4 is a simple calculation of books returned subtracted from gross books shipped. And the *fifth column* is the net number of books shipped for the single-charge columns only, that is, volumes 2 and 3.

Using the figures derived from the calculation of drop-off percentages as a start, you must go further. This will quantify the dollar amounts required for financial planning (Chart 5.4).

DEFINITIONS, EXPLANATIONS, AND OTHER KEYS

Net Sales

This figure is simply the total selling price per volume: $7.98 + $1.25 shipping = $9.23.

Chart 5.4   Pro Forma Continuity P&L: $7.98 + $1.25 per Volume

Net Sales

93.50 singles @ $9.23 = $863.01
21.25 bulks   @ $156.91 = $3334.34 $4197.35
                         Net sales: Starter $41.97

Sales and Delivery

Manufacturing	Units	Unit Cost		Total
Vol. 1, net	98.00	$ 1.25	=	$122.50
Vol. 2, net	56.00	1.25	=	70.00
Vol. 3, net	37.50	1.25	=	46.88
Bulk, net	21.25	21.25	=	451.56
Royalty				
Net charge, singles	93.50	$0.05	=	$ 4.68
Net bulk	21.25	0.85	=	18.06
Shipping and handling				
All singles, gross	220.00	$1.19	=	$261.80
Bulk, gross	25.00	5.00	=	125.00
Addnl. postage, vol. 3	50.00	0.176	=	8.80
Addnl. postage, bulk	25.00	0.161	=	4.03
Return delivery				
Single returns	28.50	$0.99	=	$28.22
Bulk returns	3.75	3.90	=	14.63
Refurbishing				
All returned books	92.25	$0.05	=	$4.61

Total sales and Delivery	$1160.77	
Overhead @ 15 percent of net sales	629.60	
Bad debt @ 20 percent of net sales	839.47	
Breakeven	$15.68	
10 percent allowable	$11.48	

Singles. Single volumes. The resulting figure is the fifth column from Chart 5.3, multiplied by $9.23.

Bulks. The net bulk shipment (column 4 of Chart 5.3) times the total price for a single bulk shipment. Here's how to arrive at the final number:
   a. The net bulk shipped (361.25) is divided by the number of books in each bulk shipment (17), which equals 21.25 net bulk books shipped.

b. *Then* multiply the 21.25 figure by the total price of a single *bulk* shipment ($9.23 × 17 books).

Finally, the total sales for singles *and* bulks are added together to reach $4197.35. This number is divided by 100—remember that we had 100 starters—to give you the net sales figure per single starter: $41.97.

Sales and Delivery

Utilizing Chart 5.3, all costs are taken into consideration.

1. **Manufacturing.** The net books shipped times the manufacturing cost of each book. The bulk cost is the same number times 17.
2. **Royalty.** Often with a book continuity series and *always* with a record continuity series, a charge for royalty is involved. It varies, but it's usually based on the net-paid sales figures. (That's the cash you've paid, after subtracting bad debt and cancellation.)
3. **Shipping and handling.** Five elements are included: outgoing postage, carton cost, inserting the book into the carton, labeling, and mailing. Chart 5.4 shows this cost reduced to a per book basis, based on *gross* shipments.
4. **Additional postage, volume 3.** As mentioned earlier, a customer can owe for two volumes (that is, volumes 2 and 3 will be shipped without a payment requirement), but at the time of shipping volume 3, some customers have paid for volume 2. With the third shipment, a statement is included requesting payment from those who have *not* paid. Since the first-class charge for the statement is 22¢ and since in this example we're assuming that 80 percent have not paid for volume 2, we charge only 80 percent of 22¢, or 17.6¢.
5. **Additional postage, bulk.** Postage charge for statement with the bulk shipment requesting payment for a second single volume. It is estimated that 73 percent of the people have not paid for both single volumes (73 percent × 22¢ = 16.1¢).
6. **Return delivery.** Cost of postage plus a handling charge for books returned. Costs will vary between a single book return and a bulk return.
7. **Refurbishing.** Cost involved (on a unit basis) for opening returned cartons, examining the book or books, and returning to inventory those that are not severely damaged.

Overhead

This figure is shown here as a percentage of net sales.

Bad Debt

This figure is shown here as a percentage of net sales.

Calculation of Allowable Breakeven

The total Sales and Delivery, Overhead, and Bad Debt ($1160.77 + $629.60 + $839.47 = $2629.84) is subtracted from the net sales and divided by 100 to arrive at breakeven per starter: ($4197.35 − $2629.84)/ 100 = $15.68.

If, for example, a particular promotion yields a CPO of $12.68, then breakeven minus CPO gives us our profit per order: $15.68 − $12.68 = $3.00 profit per order.

Ten Percent Allowable

In this example, this is the target CPO required to earn 10 percent profit on sales. To find the allowable, multiply net sales per starter by 10 percent ($41.97 × 10 percent = $4.20), and subtract this figure from the breakeven ($15.68 − $4.20 = $11.48). If orders are generated from a given promotion at $11.48, our profit would be $4.20 per order:

$$\frac{\$\ 4.20}{\$41.97} = 10 \text{ percent}$$

It is apparent in this exercise that it takes time and effort to work your way through the thinking and the math. But for every company using direct response marketing, the result is a very useful tool for financial planning. And this mode of analytical thinking is applicable to the calculations of P&L statements for book clubs, record clubs, magazines, merchandisers, etc.

OTHER EVALUATION TECHNIQUES

Income per Promotional Dollar Spent

The income per promotional dollar spent (Chart 5.5) can be considered a return on investment application. The chart shows several ways this technique can be used.

In the last calculation on the chart, for example, you have a decision criterion. You know the ultimate value of a customer over a specific period of time. Based on this factor, you can decide whether it is financially prudent to spend $1 in promotion costs even though only 76 cents in income is generated.

Chart 5.5   Income per Promotional Dollar Spent

1,300	$5.00 trials	= $ 6,500	Here we show the different price levels to calculate total income.
1,700	$9.50 full term	= $16,150	
	Total 3,000	$22,650	

$22,650 (total income) divided by
125,000 (quantity mailed) = $0.18
income per name mailed.

Income per name mailed.

$22,650 (total income) divided by
3,000 (number of responses) =
$7.55 income per response

Income per response.

$22,650 (total income) divided by
$30,000 (total cost) = $0.76
income per dollar spent (ROI).

Income per promotional dollar spent.

Each list and each total mailing are rated on this basis, which adds another perspective to the initial response. If credit was offered, bad pay from credit can be evaluated at a later point in the report because of the time lag inherent in billing procedures.

Danger in Good Results on Low Unit Offer Tests

Some publications give free issues, $1 trials, and other incentives at a loss (as introductory offers) with the objective of converting these trials to full-price subscriptions. One case study conducted on a $1 trial offer resulted in the pattern shown on Chart 5.6.

The figures indicate that initial returns from a given list are not definitive as to what will happen on conversions. For example, the list which pulled the lowest initial return was the second highest on net return and had the highest conversion percentage.

Lists which produce an exceptional return on a free or low unit offer must be checked carefully since the percentage of conversions and poor credit may make them unprofitable. On the other hand, lists which produce a low initial response may surprisingly end up with a high conversion, high pay-up rate. The characteristics and quality of the individual lists used are more important than the initial returns. To establish quality, it is essential to check returns through the conversion effort.

Free-Issue Offers

On a free first-issue magazine offer, let's take a look at some of the arithmetic to be considered in evaluating the offer. Chart 5.7 shows the net cost per subscriber figure at different levels of gross response and

Chart 5.6 Case Study Conducted on a $1 Trial Offer

List	Initial Return (Percent)	Conversion (Percent)	Net Return (Percent)
1	6.86	23	1.58
2	6.17	13	0.80
3	5.91	13	0.77
4	5.86	24	1.41
5	5.29	26	1.38
6	5.22	12	0.63
7	5.14	23	1.18
8	5.00	18	0.90
9	4.90	15	0.74
10	4.57	26	1.19
11	4.20	34	1.43

cancellations based on promotion costs only. For a net cost per subscriber of under $10, a 5 percent gross response with a 60 to 70 percent pay-up is needed. On a 4 percent gross response, a 70 percent pay-up is needed. In most free-issue situations, this high pay-up is not attainable. What this estimating process does, however, is emphasize the urgency of making a strong conversion effort and being more realistic in projecting the financing required at different levels of net response.

Target Cost per Order

Many different formulas are used to establish the maximum dollar amount that can be spent to bring in an order. Here is one example:

1. *Sales revenue* (which takes into account the persistency factor, that is, the customer value) $100
2. Less *direct costs* (cost of goods, postage, freight, storage, fulfillment)   80
3. Equals *order margin*   20
4. Less cost of money and attributable overhead   5
5. *Result*: the maximum amount that can be spent to bring in an order $ 15

Accountability Summary in Brief

The preceding examples illustrate just a few ways of determining the cost efficiency of your direct mail promotions. There is no universal formula. Financial dynamics differ among companies, but the basic truth

Chart 5.7   Free-Issue Offers:
Response Levels (Gross and Net Orders)

Gross Orders	Gross Percent Response	Gross Cost per Subscription	Percent Cancellations	Net Orders	Net Percent Response	Net Cost per Subscription
7500	5.0	$ 5.50	30	5250	3.50	$ 7.86
			40	4500	3.00	9.17
			50	3750	2.50	11.00
			60	3000	2.00	13.75
6750	4.5	6.11	30	4725	3.15	8.73
			40	4050	2.70	10.19
			50	3375	2.25	12.22
			60	2700	1.80	15.28
6000	4.0	6.88	30	4200	2.80	9.82
			40	3600	2.40	11.46
			50	3000	2.00	13.75
			60	2400	1.60	17.19
5250	3.5	7.86	30	3675	2.45	11.22
			40	3150	2.10	13.10
			50	2625	1.75	15.71
			60	2100	1.40	19.64
4500	3.0	9.17	30	3150	2.10	13.10
			40	2700	1.80	15.28
			50	2250	1.50	18.33
			60	1800	1.20	22.92
3750	2.5	11.00	30	2625	1.75	15.71
			40	2250	1.50	18.33
			50	1875	1.25	22.00
			60	1500	1.00	27.50
3000	2.0	13.75	30	2100	1.40	19.64
			40	1800	1.20	22.92
			50	1500	1.00	27.50
			60	1200	0.80	34.38
2250	1.5	18.33	30	1575	1.05	26.19
			40	1350	0.90	30.56
			50	1125	0.75	36.67
			60	900	0.60	45.83

Total test quantity: 150,000
Cost in the mail: $275/M
Total cost: $41,250

is that the management of revenues and expenses is the bottom line for all companies.

The target order cost, or allowable order cost (or whatever your company's nomenclature), is simply lifetime net revenue per customer minus all *direct* costs including promotion and provisions for overhead and cost of money and profit requirements. What remains is the amount your company would want to spend to acquire a new customer.

IMPACT OF NET-NAME ARRANGEMENT ON LIST COST

Why pay full list rental charges rather than the net charge for usable names? This has never been a simple question to answer. In the past some list owners felt that they were supplying their list *and* their information. The owner felt that full payment was required because the number of names ordered was supplied. Over time, however, list owners became somewhat more realistic. They agreed to accept a net-name arrangement based upon a fixed percentage of the number of names ordered. While the 85 percent payment seems to have developed as the standard, it is by no means cast in stone. There really is no set policy about net names, but that is part of the pleasures and problems of the free-enterprise system.

This issue is still sometimes generating more heat than light because the system has extended beyond removing duplicates to other exclusion factors: Zip codes, edit drops, three- or four-line addresses, names with first-name initials, box numbers, and others.

Chart 5.8   Comparative Costs and Percentage of Profit to Sales Based on Net-Name Arrangements

	Full Payment	**85 Percent Payment**	**Net-Net Payment**
Mail quantity	65,000	65,000	65,000
CPM	$276.92	$266.19	$251.88
Percent response	2.50%	2.50%	2.50%
Cost per order	$11.08	$10.65	$10.68
Breakeven	$13.00	$13.00	$13.00
Total profit	$3120	$3819	$4745
Percent profit on sales	6.58%	8.05%	10.00%

It is important, however, to consider the positive benefits of merge/purge: cost savings and the ability to glean some marketing information from the match rate of a list against the house file. This added dimension can clue you in to the types of lists which can be responsive. If you look at some numbers, the picture becomes more defined (Chart 5.8). The constants in Chart 5.8 are as follows:

a. 100M names are ordered.
b. 20M are eliminated by merge/purge.
c. 15M are eliminated by Zip code.
d. The *net* quantity mailed: 65,000.
e. The list user did his own Zip code elimination; the list rented at $50/M; cost in the mail was $200/M *excluding* list rental.
f. Sales: $47,450.

Explanations of the column divisions within Chart 5.8 follow:

Full-Payment Costs

65,000 @	$200/M	=	$13,000.00
100,000 @	50/M	=	5,000.00
65,000	$276.92/M		$18,000.00

85 Percent Payment
$3.50/M running charges on 15 percent of names.

65,000 @	$200.00/M	=	$13,000.00
85,000 @	50.00/M	=	4,250.00
15,000 @	3.50/M	=	52.50
65,000	$266.19/M		$17,302.50

Net-Net Payment (based on Quantity Mailed)
$3.50/M running charges for Zip code omission and duplicate names.

65,000 @	$200.00/M	=	$13,000.00
65,000 @	50.00/M	=	3,250.00
35,000 @	3.50/M	=	122.50
65,000	$251.88/M		$16,372.50

As you can see, if the goal is a 10 percent ratio of profit to sales, only the net-net name basis would pay off. Therefore, only on a net-net name basis would the mailer return to rent again.

While it is essential that the percentage of response to a list be considered, actually more importance should be paid to the cost to secure the customer. Package, production, and postage costs remain consistent for a mailing, but the order cost will vary according to the actual list price as determined by a net-name arrangement. This is one "variable" that is controlled by the list owner and can represent the difference between a successful list that will be used consistently or one that will be dropped.

In the long run other options must be considered. As list universes and the size of mailings increase, the rate of duplication will also increase. With Zip code and other eliminations also a factor, the usable quantity will decrease. If a list can be made to work on a net-net name basis only, that's probably the only way a mailer will order, and list owners are going to have to live with that fact. What must be considered? If mailers can only use a list on a net-net name basis, how will this impact list rental income for the list owner? List owners should keep a record of these "turned off" orders in order to get a clear view of lost income. Would a small increase in the base list rental price compensate for a net-net arrangement?

See Chart 5.9 for further emphasis on the difference in list costs after merge/purge versus the basic list rental charge. You will note that the actual list rental cost swings from $46.33 to $72.00 per thousand names, which is a significant difference.

Effect of Overkill on List Costs

Some companies retain match code tapes of previous mailings, and this can create a problem. In one example, merging the March tape versus the previous January mailing resulted in a loss of 50 percent of the names. This suppression caused two problems: (1) There was a substantial increase in list rental cost, and (2) in order to meet subscription requirements, it was necessary to include a substantial quantity from marginal lists which resulted in a further cost increase.

A 50 percent loss translates roughly into doubling the list costs. In this instance, the list cost became $80 to $90/M rather than $40 to $45. Consider how many orders are needed to cover the $40 to $45/M cost increase. This led to a decision to test what would happen if the names mailed *60 days* previously were included. The result was that the inclusion of names mailed 60 days previously had no significant effect on response. On subsequent mailings, however, response did decrease. But on an overall cost-per-order basis, the decrease in response did not have as severe an impact as it would have had if marginal lists had been added.

This observation is certainly worth testing by including a cell of the normally suppressed names and unique names combined versus a cell of "pure" names (omitting the names normally suppressed under the 60−90 day system). The results should be compared on a response and order cost basis. The list cost will impact the latter. Sometimes this overkill of prior usage can be counterproductive especially in relatively vertical markets.

Direct mail grew dramatically over decades when it was not practical to remove duplicates. Yet today some mailers go to great expense to omit names used as far back as 9 to 12 months. Should direct marketers let the fact that direct mail is measurable make them so gun-shy that the appraisal is on a campaign-*by*-campaign basis? Should we not explore the interaction of elements on a campaign-*to*-campaign basis? For instance, the principle of frequency is a highly accepted practice in general adver-

Chart 5.9 Actual List Cost per Thousand after Merge/Purge

Gross Quantity	List Cost per Thousand	Running Charges per Thousand	Selection Charges per Thousand	Billing				
				85 Percent on Basic List Rental	Running Costs	Selection Charges	Total Billing	Actual List CPM
50,000	$40.00	$5.00	—	$1,700.00	$37.50	—	$1,737.50	$46.33
50,000	40.00	5.00	$6.50	1,700.00	37.50	$325.00	2,062.50	55.00
50,000	45.00	5.00	—	1,912.50	37.50	—	1,950.00	52.00
50,000	45.00	5.00	4.50	1,912.50	37.50	225.00	2,175.00	58.00
50,000	50.00	5.00	—	2,125.00	37.50	—	2,162.50	57.67
50,000	50.00	5.00	7.50	2,125.00	37.50	375.00	2,537.50	67.67
50,000	55.00	5.00	—	2,337.50	37.50	—	2,375.00	63.33
50,000	55.00	5.00	6.50	2,337.50	37.50	325.00	2,700.00	72.00

Constants: 25 percent duplication; 37,500 mailed.

tising. In direct mail this premise could be systematically studied, perhaps not in mass markets but certainly in well-defined markets. In other words, how often can you mail to the same names?

MORE ABOUT MERGE/PURGE

Over the past 2 decades technology has significantly enhanced the effectiveness of direct mail in a variety of ways. One of the first was the ability to maintain lists on the computer. This led to duplication control as computer merge/purge systems were developed. There are many excellent systems with added dimensions beyond just identifying duplicates to marketing-decision support.

However, there have been problems in the allocation of payments to list owners because of the input methodology used in merge/purge. Some mailers use a priority system which depends on previous response; i.e., the list which pulled the highest response (1.8 percent) goes in first and so on. Others use a first-come (delivery of tapes), first-in basis, while some use a random system.

There is a self-perpetuating bias in the first methodology mentioned. The others are random and less biased. One important principle to follow is to give test lists priority. If the tests are put in at the bottom, chances are, particularly on a large mailing, that the quantity mailed could be too small for statistical response measurement.

ALLOCATION OF PAYMENTS TO LIST OWNERS

One constant problem which emerges, no matter the procedure, is the calculation of payment to the list·owner. The net-payment routine which follows (Appendix 5A) shows the necessary data on which calculations can be based. This procedure has many possible variations and applications, but it does serve as a guide toward identifying the critical components of the calculation process.

APPENDIX 5A

A Method for Allocating Payments to List Owners

Here is one method of calculating equitable net payments to list owners if the contributing lists contain multinames for which credit has to be distributed to more than one owner.

Each file will be subjected to the usual reformation pass during which intrafile duplicates will be removed and a *blank control field* (described below) will be added to each name record. The only problem remaining is to perform the interfile purging and to compute the true contribution of the individual lists to the final mailing list.

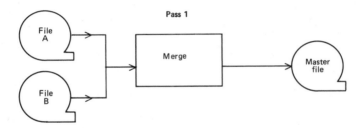

The first two files (A and B) are merged into a master file. The master file will have a control field attached to each name record with the following layout:

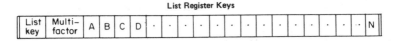

List key. Indicating the code of the list under which this name will be mailed

Multifactor. A two-digit numeric subfield indicating the number of lists this name was on

List register keys. *N* number of one-digit subfield where *N* equals the total number of contributing lists

When comparing a name on list A with list B, if the name is found on list A only, the list key will be made A, the multifactor will be increased by 1, and the register key for A will be turned on. If the name is on list B only, the list key will be made B, the multifactor will be increased by 1, and the register key for B will be turned on. If the name is on both lists, the list key will be made A, the multifactor will be increased by 2, and the register key for both A and B will be turned on.

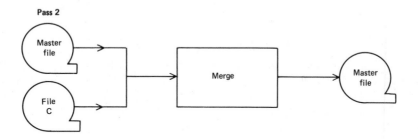

The master file and file C are then merged into a new master. If the name is on the master only, the record is passed as is. At this point, proceed to the next name.

If the name is on file C only, it will go on the master file, the list key will be made C, the multifactor will be increased by 1, and the register key for C will be turned on. Passes 3 through $N - 2$ will be identical to pass 2.

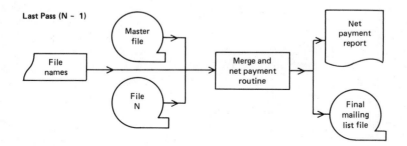

Before passing each record to the final mailing list file, the net-payment computing routine is performed. The register keys are no longer required and may be dropped from the final mailing list file if reformatting is feasible. At the end of the job, a net-payment report is printed. The names of the files can be entered on cards.

NET PAYMENT ROUTINE

During the last pass, the name control field for each final record will typically look like this:

Name Control Register

Note that V means that the key is *on*. The list key is C (mailed under C). The name appeared on five lists, namely, C, E, H, K, and M.

Prior to the last pass, a *master list register field* is established with the following layout:

Master List Register

List A	Net payment	List B	Net payment	List C	Net payment	List D	Net payment	List E	}{	List M	Net payment	List N	Net payment

The calculation of the contribution of each list is made by dividing each name by the multifactor on the name record (1/5 in the example) and crediting that amount to the net-payment field of every list whose register key is *on*.

List Net Pay   Master List Register

After completion of the last pass (pass $N - 1$), the sum of net payments will equal the total number of names mailed, and the net payment for every contributing list will represent the true contribution of each list to the final mailing list.

This equitable payment method would make the following side benefits available to the list rental customer;

1. Statistical information about the effectiveness of multinames over singles
2. Statistical information about the effectiveness of the contributing lists

Knowing the multiplicity factor of each name, the following table can be readily developed:

	Number of Names Mailed	Multifactor	
	1,234,000	01	(Names on one list only)
	325,000	02	(Names on two lists)
	168,000	03	(Names on three lists)
	73,000	04	(Names on four lists)
Total	1,800,000		

EFFECTIVENESS OF MULTINAMES

Suppose that the mailing to 1 million names generated 74,000 replies. If the multifactor is keyed into the address label, Table A can be generated:

Table A

Number of Names Mailed	Multifactor	Number of Responses	Percent Response
1,234,000	01	42,000	3.40
325,000	02	16,000	4.92
168,000	03	10,500	6.25
73,000	04	5,500	7.53
1,800,000		74,000	4.11

Table A can be obtained without extra cost to mailers, and it should be of some value to them, particularly because the likelihood of obtaining similar ratios between responses to the mailings in various multifactor groups with another set of lists is rather high.

EFFECTIVENESS OF THE CONTRIBUTING LISTS

To compute the effectiveness of the contributing lists, only the names in multifactor group 01 should be used. Assuming that the list code and the multifactor are keyed onto the address label, Table B can be developed. In the example, five lists were used—A, B, C, D, and E.

Table B

List Name	Number of Names Mailed with Multifactor 01	Number of Responses with Multifactor 01	Percent Response
A	255,000	8,500	3.33
B	243,000	6,700	2.76
C	246,000	7,900	3.21
D	236,000	8,400	3.56
E	254,000	10,500	4.13
	1,234,000	42,000	3.40

The information in both Tables A and B can be used effectively to formulate future mailing strategies.

CHAPTER 6

Customer File: The Rich Vein of Profits

The marketing concept is central to every business's main purpose: attracting and retaining customers. Customers are a company's most valuable asset. *The best customer is the one you already have*. It follows then that cultivating that customer, knowing that customer, satisfying that customer, and retaining that customer will lead to the incremental sales necessary on your pathway to profits. If it is true that, in the sports world, the fans *make* the team, then in direct marketing, the customers *are* the team.

The ideal situation in direct mail is to match the product or offer with the prospect most likely to respond. The chances of doing this are infinitely better with your customer list than with any other because, potentially, you have the most knowledge about your own customers. Effective targeting of the customer data base can be achieved only through:

1. Complete understanding of your customer universe and the segments within the total universe
2. The development and application of techniques for isolating these segments.

Direct marketing companies do not have a single mailing list. They have many. How many? Only segmentation will tell. The opportunities to segment the customer file into marketing units with purchasing behavioral characteristics are vast. While this analysis is obviously handled more efficiently and precisely by computer technology and mathematical applications, it doesn't preclude a small business with a small list from using the basic principles in a manual application.

With a data base structure you can develop information by systematic analysis of customer transactional data. This will help you determine the customer's propensity to respond to specific promotions by identifying and scoring the attributes (type of product purchased, source, seasons, etc.) which appear to have the most impact on customer behavior. These activity patterns can create the building blocks necessary for successful marketing intelligence, which will lead to better deployment of this important asset. Think of your data base as the seismograph of your business.

ADVANTAGES OF SEGMENTATION

The concept of segmentation is not new. Ancient business practitioners may not have recognized "segmentation" as a concept, but they used it instinctively by selling different wares at different prices to kings and to peasants. This was the use of demography to distinguish their market segments, simply, the rich and the poor. Obviously, this basic distinction is too simplistic and no longer a given segmentation technique. *Another fact:* The people who buy your product or service are different from those who don't. Simplistic? Yes, but this is the basis for the theory of market segmentation, a concept which can be used to classify people on the basis of characteristics which appear to affect the purchase of your product or service or, in the case of fund raising, the characteristics which affect the contribution to the charitable cause.

By dividing your customer base into segments, you can design your promotion to appeal to those people with the highest propensity to respond. If you know the composition of your file, you will be in a better position to predict who will buy and even to influence purchase decisions. Market researchers have already predicted the demise of mass marketing. "Demassification" is no longer a buzzword; it's a marketing reality. The consumer can no longer be considered as unitarian and monolithic.

Purchase decisions are the result of the interplay of many factors, some of which are beyond the direct marketer's control. However, that old axiom "knowledge is power" is taking on a powerful, fresh meaning for direct marketers. Purchasing pattern recognition should not be a formula-driven technique which relates only to the past. What is needed is a system with the ability to observe patterns and trends, a sense of the road ahead, since we live in a world of unprecedented change.

In broad terms, then, the objective is to add more value to the customers already on the books by segmenting that audience into more precise, identifiable, and predictable units.

WHERE DO YOU START?

You begin by listening to your customers. Every time a purchase is made, a personal statement is being made. Every time a customer makes a payment, writes a letter, returns a product, changes address, doesn't pay a bill, etc., you have transactional data. Even a complaint can be an opportunity if treated as a channel of communication rather than an annoyance. It's how this information is captured, analyzed, and used that counts.

It is not the intention here to go into the design of the system but rather to emphasize the necessity for a system that will make it possible to see the forest and the trees. Understanding what consumers may want is apt to keep marketers busy for years. The reward ratio will be higher for those companies who understand the consumer's commitment to an individual mode of existence, who can address this aspect, and who can put it to work for them.

The changes in demographic and societal trends (psychographics) are not only identifiable but can also be inferred and pinpointed by activity, but only if the proper descriptors are included in the data base. As business becomes more information-driven, the ability to access information from the data base assumes primary importance.

Let's consider the meaning of some of the terminology. *Data* means factual information used as a basis for reasoning, discussion, or calculation. *Information* is knowledge communicated or received concerning a particular fact or circumstance. *Data base* refers to computerized methods of storing and processing large amounts of data. *Data bank* refers to a collection of data organized especially for rapid search and retrieval. *Information retrieval* is the systematic recovery of data, for example, from a file or from the memory bank of a computer.

GATHERING, UNDERSTANDING, AND USING INFORMATION

By the early years of this century, the big mail-order merchants were sending out anywhere from 2 to 13 million catalogs a year. Even in those low-cost, cheap postage days, that represented a pretty big up-front expense. At some point before World War I, the mail-order companies developed the "12-month prune." This symbolic term, borrowed from the horticulturalists, literally means "to trim off superfluous branches."

This is the way it worked. You simply sat your clerks down once a year with an alphabetized order file and your mailing list. If you couldn't find an order within the past year from Alfred P. Adams of Muskogee, Oklahoma, you crossed the name off the mailing list. Obviously, he wasn't a good customer. This was an erroneous conclusion, as it turned out, because it left too many gaps and still didn't guarantee a profit from everyone who received a catalog.

If you've ever seen one of the reproductions of the old Sears or Ward catalogs that were produced as "nostalgia" items several years ago, you know that they were about the size of today's Brooklyn telephone directory. If you mailed one to Adams every year and all that was ordered was one shirt, the fact that Adams was an *active* customer under the 12-month system didn't mean that you were making a profit. Conversely, if you dropped Adams from 1911 mailing because of no purchase activity in 1910, your competitor might end up selling the Adams family a new kitchen range or overcoats for their two children. What was needed, then, was a method to enable the prediction of purchasing potential.

THE RECENCY, FREQUENCY, MONETARY METHOD OF CONTROLLING CIRCULATION

In the decade from 1930 to 1940, a period of low profits, low average order, and relatively low sales volume, the large mail-order companies of America made a major move in the areas of cost reduction to arrest the decline of what was considered, at that time, to be a waning industry. This move was outstandingly successful in reducing costs, but its total effect was much more far-reaching than anticipated. In fact, it was probably the force that revolutionized the industry from all the important business points of view—profits, sales volume, acceptance by the public, and continued expansion.

This extraordinary step was actually only a formalizing and measurement of a mass of half-thought-out and half-understood information long suspected or known by many mail-order people. Bits and pieces of it had been used for a quarter of a century before but never effectively. When fully developed, it was given the awkward and fearsome title "The *R*ecency, *F*requency, *M*onetary Method of Controlling Circulation," which was abbreviated to RFM.

Essentially, this technique of controlling circulation is the same in principle as the insurance companies' actuarial method of rating risks. In brief, it estimates from the past buying performance of categories of customers over a period of time (2 years or four 6-month seasons) how much these categories will buy. If the sales expected from a reading of these correlated standards is too small in relation to the cost, the category is not mailed.

In the original studies, the elements or standards which controlled 90 percent of the reasons why customers repeat at a certain sales volume were found to be (1) *recency* of the last order or orders before mailing, (2) *frequency* (whether a single or multiple) of ordering performance in the four seasons before mailing, and (3) *monetary value* of the order or orders in a given season. The weighing of these factors in the total value of 90 percent of all factors was broadly:

Frequency: 50 of 90 percent

Recency: 35 of 90 percent

Monetary: 15 of 90 percent

In brief, a customer category which ordered within the last 6 months before mailing (recency) and sent two or more orders during that period (frequency) for a combined total of over $100 (monetary) was just about the cream of the list. Conversely, a customer category which had ordered in the 6- to 12-month period before mailing and sent only one order for a total of less than $10 was probably the poorest segment of the list. The superiority of the first group mentioned over the second could be as high as 10 to 1. In between, there were as many as 50 categories of varying qualities, all of whose repeat business could be reduced to a cost-reward ratio, in other words, profitable or unprofitable and thus mailed or not mailed. If a company had established its break-even profit point on cost-to-sales ratio (based on markup and operating costs), it tended to mail all categories where the selling ratio was lower than breakeven and not mail to those with a selling ratio higher than breakeven. As someone so aptly put it, you picked them by their batting averages.

This circulation control method enabled mail-order companies to reduce their mailings by from 40 to 55 percent without loss of profitable business. Thus the largest mail-order company reduced the circulation of its 1000+-page catalog mailed twice a year from 13 million to between 7 and 8 million and the second largest from 11 million to from 6 to 6.5 million. Others cut circulation even more, percentage-wise. The savings were obviously enormous, and it was these savings that triggered the renaissance of the mail-order business in the late thirties, a movement that has continued to the present day.

RFM was a tremendous beginning and still a valid measurement, but it was perhaps just the tip of the iceberg. In this age of electronic brains, it is possible to add to this mathematical correlation of controlling circulation. Each company must isolate its own interdynamic factors from which conclusions can be reached. Remember that the original RFM method defined factors for 90 percent of the problem. At this point, it seems reasonable to assume that technology has accounted for the remaining 10 percent by using a different set of criteria based on the product or service being offered.

EXTENSION OF DISCRIMINANTS

Let's take a look at some general discriminants, in addition to recency, frequency, and monetary, that can be considered in the building of the data base.

1. **Sex.** prefix: Mr., Ms., Mrs., Miss, Mr. and Mrs.
2. **Address.** street or box number.
3. **City, state, Zip code.**
4. **Date of entry on file.**
5. **Type of product purchased.** Labeled by categories such as household, leisure, recreation, fashions, gourmet, travel, sports, do-it-yourself, children's, and pet. And within these broad labels, an expansion into a definition of discretionary versus trendy versus utilitarian versus unit of sale. The affluent group might consider a trendy item a reflection of their standards. A lower-income prospect might consider the item "wasteful." For example, sunglasses used to be inexpensive and utilitarian, but recently expensive sunglasses selling from $100 to $1900 a pair captured about 40 percent of the market in 1983. Trend or fad? Only monitoring will tell. However, the purchase of a food processor, exotic herbs, or an exercise machine is a trend and not a fad. In other words, this is the type of data that would enhance the *psychographic profile.*
6. **Source.** Direct mail by *category* of list used. Space by media type (specific interest magazines, news magazines, regional magazines, newspapers, etc.). TV, cable, radio by the programming environment of the commercial. Telephone by offer, direct solicitation, lead follow-up, type of list used.
7. **Seasonality.** While there are financial and other considerations relative to the mailing period, seasonality does impact response. It is

essential that a correlation be drawn between the date of entry on the file, offer, source, and customer performance. For example, does the customer who comes on the file as a result of a Christmas promotion behave the same way as a customer who responded to an offer at other times of the year? A seasonality study by product categories (see Appendix 8A) demonstrates seasonal variations.

8. **Offer.** A *hard offer* means that no discount, short-term trial, free-issue, sweepstakes, or any other inducement device was used. A *soft offer* indicates that an introductory inducement has been used. If a premium was used, note whether the premium was sent after payment was received or upon receipt of the order.

9. **Mode of payment.** Cash (check or money order), charge account (with the company), COD, installment purchase, credit card. Note whether the credit card is one of the travel and entertainment cards such as American Express Green and Gold cards, Diners Club, or Carte Blanche or a more general card such as Visa or Mastercard.

10. **Recency of last transaction.** Purchase, renewal, payment, address change, merchandise return, complaint.

11. **Geographics.** The movement of people has made geodynamics an important part of segmentation; geographical mobility does impact markets. Population redistribution is ongoing, and knowing where your markets were last year does not mean they will be in the same place this year or next.

12. **Length of time on file.** Persistency. The indisputable sign of a loyal and valued customer or, conversely, the looker, the one-time buyer.

To some degree, these suggestions are intended to overcome the weakness with most statistics. They are not society-oriented. In other words, numbers alone can't reveal the effect on your marketing in the more mobile lifestyles evidenced by the societal changes that have impacted and will continue to impact the market place. You must set up the mechanism that will.

One way would be to use precise source codes which are more than just numbers. For example, a particular letter code could designate the type of list used, the category of the magazine used, or the program environment of the TV, cable, or radio spots. If these letter codes were constant, experience could be accumulated on the types of media and/or the type of list producing the most response, the most revenue, the most incremental business, etc.

To expand on this coding system as it relates to direct mail, here are three major areas which can be considered in setting up a list usage coding system:

1. **Type of list.** Magazines, books, book clubs, record clubs, newsletters, credit cards, merchandise, donors, compilations (business, consumer, associations)
2. **Subject matter.** Business-oriented, investments and financial planning, sports and hobbies, science and technology, home interest and entertaining, cultural interest, self-improvement, nature and outdoors, health and fitness, history and current events
3. **Segmentation.** Hotline, changes of address, source, gender, actives, expires, inquiry, geographics

There are many other possibilities, but these standards would cover 80 to 90 percent of the fundamentals needed to make more responsible decisions on the selection of lists to be tested and how to test them.

The other extremely important part of the segmentation process is the methodology which will be used in analyzing and correlating this vast amount of data. Bring the statisticians and mathematicians in at the beginning so that the system design will be synchronized with the desired marketing objectives.

With today's computerized records, a company can key all promotions to develop more definitive data on any person who buys. What is being suggested is a concept to expand the application of data, for profiling purposes.

For example, we know something potentially valuable about a customer's interest the moment we identify that person as someone who reads a sports, shelter, hobby, historical, or any category magazine; who lives in Maine or Michigan but reads the Sunday *New York Times*; who's been a customer for audio equipment, specialized books, or furniture kits; who listens to classical music, rock, or jazz or watches panel shows or movies on TV. Can't we describe this as a harmonization of data elements?

The optimally efficient subgroup to be selected as the mailing list must not be so tight as to cut off too many fringe sections with sizable quantities of potential customers nor so broad as to bring in an outer fringe with so few potential customers as to be uneconomic. Methods for doing this are complicated and can spawn a new and growing specialty. As a kind of amalgam of psychology, economics, and mathematics, let's call it "population analysis."

The advantages of population analysis to the seller are obvious, but it is a service to the potential customer as well. To eliminate a person from those mailing lists to which her or his chance of responding is poor has an advantage also. That person will be removed from that aspect of direct mail advertising which is most irritating, i.e., getting offers which are of no interest.

HOW DO CUSTOMERS
RATE YOUR SERVICE?

Direct marketing loses its raison d'être—convenience—if a customer has to write, call, argue, or check several times in order to solve a problem. Supermarkets have found that people are more concerned with long lines than price. Isn't that an indication that service—fulfillment—is an important ingredient in the direct marketing process?

Customer service, an integral part of the entire direct marketing process, must begin with the customer's evaluation. This direct action is the only way to carefully appraise the service problems that cost your company sales or, conversely, to help improve an already effective system. The old adage "if it ain't broke, don't fix it" doesn't mean that you can't improve it even if it isn't broken. There are various methods which can be used to collect customer feedback. Mail surveys are probably the most inexpensive research method (approximately $1.50 to $1.75 per questionnaire) and also the fastest for securing a large number of responses. Telephone inquiries and personal interviews generate more extensive information but are much more expensive than mail surveys.

Another approach to consider would be to include an analysis vehicle with the shipment of, for example, merchandise, books, or records, to capture a marketing profile. A dollar credit toward the next purchase could stimulate a higher response.

Whichever research methodology is used, the most important criterion is the extraction of the customer sample. For example, if dollar amount of purchases is decided as the major criterion upon which decisions will be based, then the 20 percent of your customers that account for 80 percent of your sales should comprise most of the sample.

The survey should be so designed that the customer can rank in order of importance the various components of the customer service system, i.e., delivery time, order status, inquiries, handling of complaints, packaging, and so forth. The rating system can either be numerical (a scale of 1 to 10) or a scale of "excellent," "good," "fair," or "poor."

CUSTOMER RETENTION: USING
CUSTOMER ACTIVITY AS A
BUSINESS OPPORTUNITY

Let's consider another aspect in our concern with making direct marketing more effective and, therefore, more profitable. There are many good reasons for mailers to seek new customers and to seek advice on how to find them through careful list selection.

But there is one *bad* reason for the search. Consider how many customers become former customers each year that could have been retained with a bit more care. Customer actions tell you more than their words. In the total picture, as important as why people buy is why former customers have left. Some customers, for example, will return merchandise they find unsatisfactory or write letters of complaint about goods or service. But others, especially if the amount of money involved is not large, will simply resolve never to buy from that mailer again.

If your products are all in a single category, limited, say, to a particular interest or activity, it may be that a customer will need no new merchandise for a year or two but might resume buying in the future. Simply to drop such customers from your list would be a great mistake. Yet this is done each year as mailers routinely "clean" their lists of names that have produced no orders during a certain period of time.

When you consider the high cost of obtaining new customers, a sense of good business asks why you should not make some simple effort to retain the old ones. Before dropping a customer who has stopped ordering, why not communicate in a friendly way, expressing concern at having apparently lost a valued friend. The letter could be personalized in a way to demonstrate recognition of the customer's purchasing interests, or the letter could invite the customer to report any case in which the mailer's goods or service might have displeased the customer so that the complaint can be satisfied.

A simple, personalized form letter can accomplish two things. Obviously, it can often keep on the file a good customer who might otherwise have been dropped prematurely. It can also yield valuable marketing and product information and a means to segment your list of former customers.

After all, why is it logical to talk to a house list as though it's a new untested one? Most mailers have discovered that if they recognize a present or past customer as such, their mail pulls measurably better. Smart mailers recognize that there are gradations of customers—new, old, frequent, infrequent, big money buyers, small money buyers—each representing a customer unit requiring different promotional treatment. Effective direct marketing is a continuum. Your message must be reinforced at every point of customer contact.

Case in point: Most circulation directors call an effort to get a renewal for the first time a "conversion." And the effort to acquire the second, third, or fourth a "renewal." The difference in terminology is important; it recognizes the *difference* between the two groups.

The most important difference is that, to convert a new subscriber takes more resell than to renew an old one. Special copy is written; special offers invented for each group. *Why?* Because it's a simple fact of publishing life that first-time subscribers don't convert as well as long-time readers renew. Considering the high acquisition cost of replacing any subscriber, increasing renewals or conversions by even 1 percent does pay off handsomely on the bottom line.

SKEWED DISTRIBUTION

In most instances, skewed distribution is a reality, not a perception. It's a method necessary to identify the "core" group. Let's take a situation where a not-so-new statistical technique called "quintile analysis" was used to identify the revenue stream. The file was divided into five revenue segments (quintiles): top 20 percent, next 20 percent, and so on. This analysis was based on unit of sale, but the same application could be based on any factor or factors peculiar or important to a particular company.

It turned out in this analysis that 77 percent of the revenues were produced by the top 20 percent. This identification of the "optimum" stream yielded the necessary information on where to spend promotional dollars for maximum return. It also stimulated offers and promotional appeal to groups in the lower quintiles to try to raise income from these groups.

A uniform policy becomes a fiction when distributions such as these occur and are not recognized. Those companies that understand the *leverage* of skewed distribution or the optimum revenue stream or their own measurement criteria have statistics which measure this leverage and use it as part of strategic planning.

DATA BASE ENHANCEMENT

There are two good reasons to explore data base (internal files) enhancement:

1. To market internal products more efficiently
2. To generate additional list rental income

Internally or externally, one of the first enhancement methods used was analysis by Sectional Center Facility (SCF), the first three digits of the Zip code and five-digit Zip codes, both of which were designed by the U.S. Postal Service to facilitate mail handling and delivery. SCF also resulted in economies for companies using bulk mail. SCF analysis is not really valid for marketing purposes because of the very large areas it covers. With approximately 39,000 Zip codes across the United States, Zip code analysis is a helpful marketing tool but far from an exact science. Zip codes were designed for the convenience of mail delivery; they were not designed to be homogeneous or statistical units. Most are much too large and heterogeneous to be used aggressively in segmentation applications. For example, the Zip code for Scarsdale, New York, one of the highest-income areas in the country, includes surrounding areas from adjacent communities which do not have the same level of income, housing characteristics, or educational levels as Scarsdale.

What has developed are smaller statistical units based on census data such as block groups and enumeration districts (215,000+); census tracts (44,000 approximately); and carrier routes (approximately 180,000). Some of the evaluators used are: age, sex, marital status, family composition, family size, occupation of household head, education of household head, family income, home ownership, car ownership, ethnicity, and religion.

However, the small population in most of these units resulted in the "clustering" technique in order to create larger population groups on which to base analysis. For example, a Zip code representing a *suburban* area in metropolitan New York with primarily professional, managerial, and high-income residents living in single-family dwelling units would be combined with similar communities in suburban Chicago, Atlanta, Boston, Los Angeles, etc.

There are several companies that offer the capability of analyzing the customer files based on these ingredients. This technique is known as "overlay." It involves matching a statistically valid sample from the internal file (or the entire file) against a household data base.

To demonstrate this clustering application, let's look at PRIZM. PRIZM is a consumer market segmentation system developed over a decade ago by Claritas Corporation. Claritas developed the term "geodemography" to describe the use of census demographic and socioeconomic data at the neighborhood level of geography.

The Bureau of the Census reports over 1000 different statistics which describe the populations of neighborhoods. These variables fall essentially into five broad categories: affluence and social status, household composition, race and ethnic background, mobility, and population density and housing characteristics.

Claritas computer analyzed this vast compilation of geodemographic data and was able to classify all the neighborhoods in the United States into 40 neighborhood types or clusters. After intensive study, a "nickname" was created for each to capture its essential qualities and facilitate memory. Here are some examples: Blue Blood Estates, Money and Brains, Young Influentials, Young Suburbia, God's Country, Urban Gold Coast, Blue-Collar Nursery, Bunker's Neighbors, Old Brick Factories, Marlboro Country, Back-Country Folks, and Hard Scrabble.

This type of penetration study yields the percentage of all available households of a given type that a marketer has on the internal file and is useful as an extension of the information necessary to answer the question, "Who is my customer?" But remember that this technique is not absolute, it is directional.

The data card (e.g., Chart 6.1) shows the various selections which are available through a file overlay. But bear in mind that these characteristics, in most instances, are not available on an individual basis but inferred, based on averages or median within the measurement unit used by the data company.

A similar type of analysis is offered to business-to-business marketers by Dun's Marketing and Market Data Retrieval. This overlay, obviously, relates to companies by sales, number of employees, net worth, specific types of business by Standard Industrial Classification, occupational levels, etc.

Some of the companies also providing these services:

Donnelly Marketing Information Services, Stamford, Connecticut

R. L. Polk, Taylor, Michigan

Metromail, Lincoln, Nebraska

Wiland, Fredericksburg, Virginia

Lifestyle Selector, Denver, Colorado

Demographic Research Co., Santa Monica, California

CACI, New York City

ComSelect, Consumer Direct, Des Plaines, Illinois

EXAMPLE OF AN INTERNAL BUSINESS DATA BASE

In terms of current common usage, a "data base" is a merged group of lists with duplication removed which can be accessed by a number of variables.

One such frequently used data base is McGraw-Hill Business Leaders consisting of 1,603,556 executives. This list is a combined unduplicated file of subscribers to 18 McGraw-Hill publications. It's a good example of a data base because of the size and the degree of segmentation (Chart 6.2).

Let's look at the selections offered. The first is by industry based on the U.S. Department of Commerce Standard Industrial Classification codes (SIC). The benefits are obvious. If you're promoting machinery designed for use by a construction company, you can make that selection. Another

Chart 6.1 *Fingerhut:* Merchandise Catalog

3,152,885	Paid installment buyers (1984)	@ $45/M	*Minimum: 10,000*
675,000	Hotline (monthly)	@ $45/M	
135,000	Change of address (monthly)	@ $45/M	
1,968,338	Catalog buyers (1984)	@ $50/M	
300,000	Sweeps no's (monthly)	@ $38/M	

Data   Items include auto seat covers, cookware, luggage, blankets, flatware, stereos, etc.

Unit $50 average; select multibuyers @ $5/M.   *Sample required*

Sex   70% women; select @ $2.50/M; select age @ $2.50/M.

Media   100% direct mail.

Filed   Zip sequence; 4-up Cheshire; 9T/1600 Magtape.
State / SCF / Zip @ $2.50/M.
(Zip tape conversion: $25 flat) P/S labels @ $3/M.
Keying (to 6 digits) @ N/C.
P/S labels @ $3/M.
Running charges @ $3.50/M.

Fingerhut Merchandise Credit Buyers; Select @ $2.50/M

Product selection	1984	1983	Sex select	1984	1983
Apparel	760,800	823,330	Male	320,230	534,317
Tool and auto accessories	87,382	71,491	Female	1,447,997	1,065,872
Home furnishings	1,050,754	1,408,478			
Recreation and leisure	495,198	462,682			
High-priced merchandise	316,790	228,633	*Multiple buyers*	955,328	1,066,762
Cash buyers	495,477	927,308			
			Single buyers	313,016	857,510
Income selection (by dollar range)					
High: $17,000 and over	312,005	523,545			
Med.: $11,000−$16,000	649,168	986,263	*Age select (Zip overlay)*		
Low: $10,999 and under	346,837	488,506	25−34	1,308	1,998
			35−44	327,003	499,578
Income selection (by SCF index)			45−54	954,847	1,458,769
A = Highest 20%	255,070	423,931	55 and over	5,232	7,993
B = Above average	245,307	386,294			
C = Average	266,257	414,386			
D = Below average	270,617	405,324			
E = Lowest 20%	257,490	350,145			
Neilsen markets					
A = Top 25 metros	388,659	580,146			
B = 150,000 and over	363,770	561,335			
C = 35,000−149,000	279,858	434,904			
D = Under 35,000	266,769	410,138			

**Chart 6.2   McGraw-Hill Business Leaders:
Subscribers, McGraw-Hill Publications**

1,603,556	U.S. executives	@ $63/M	
42,000	Canadian executives	@ $63/M	
123,917	Foreign executives	@ $160/M	
75,000	Women executives	@ $73/M	*Minimum: $350*

See Reverse for Additional Information

Data	Unduplicated master to *Amer. Machinist, Architectural Record, Aviation Week & Space Tech., Bus. Week, Chem. Eng., Chemical Week, Coal Age, Const. Methods & Equip., Electronic Construction & Maintenance, Electrical World, Electronics, Engineering & Mining Jrnl., Eng. News Record, House & Home, Modern Packaging, Mod. Plastics, Natl. Petroleum News, Purchasing Week.* Median age 44; 64% invest in stocks; 91% own credit cards.	*Sample required*
Sex	95% male.	
Media	Direct mail.	
Filed	Zip sequence; 4-up Cheshire; 9T/1600 Magtape.	
	Nth name @ N/C. State; SCF @ N/C. Zip @ $6/M.	*Nonreturnable*
	Keying @ $4/M. P/S labels @ $10/M.	*magtape*
	Running charges @ 9/M. Select title, company @ $6/M.	*@ $20/reel*
Note:	On orders cancelled after mail date, list owner will charge full price.	
Note:	List owner requirement: Computer-run counts in advance $9/M ($100 minimum).	

Select home/business address @ $6/M:
Business: 893,525   Home: 710,031

Select by function @ $6/M:

Top management	Marketing sales
Middle management	Other
Engineering/technical	

Select by industry / SIC @ $6/M:

Manufacturing	Wholesaling	Research and development
Construction	Services	Government
Mining	Finance	Miscellaneous
Retailing	Education	

excellent segment is job function, enabling the mailer to target the proper level of management for the purchase decision relative to the product or service being offered.

Size of company is an important segment of particular interest to business-to-business direct marketers. If your business is setting up pension plans, your approach would need to differentiate between a company with under 50 employees versus the company with 1000+ employees.

The home versus business address adds another important dimension since you now can approach the business person as a consumer. If you're selling quality men's clothing, a local sporting event, or a subscription to a personal finance service, the home address is important. Work-related solicitations such as business supplies or seminars are more successful when mailed to the business address.

Geographical selections are useful to seminar mailers who want to solicit attendees to a meeting or conference in specific locations. This also has application for lead generation for regional sales offices or for any company which has analyzed response patterns and determined that certain regions of the country are more responsive to their particular appeal than others.

Gender selection is very meaningful as women assume decision-making executive positions. With tremendous growth in recent years in the number of magazines, seminars, and investment programs geared to females, this list of 74,000 women executives represents an attractive market.

The Small Town Business Leaders are unique in their need for contact with the media centers of the United States. This segment tends to be responsive to business information in the form of books, subscriptions, seminars, and cassettes.

Owners and partners can come from companies of all sizes, but those particular titles tend to appear more frequently in smaller firms. Being entrepreneurial makes them receptive to their counterparts in the Small Town Business Leaders segment.

This ability to target into a large list is what target marketing is all about.

KNOWING YOUR CUSTOMERS IS NOT A TRIVIAL PURSUIT

The objective of any company is profits. But it is important to realize that a company can't get so wrapped up in business and profits that it forgets the customer. It is a fact that profitability is greatly affected by customer satisfaction. In direct marketing, incremental sales to the customers you already have *is* the bottom line. It has been noted that a company reaps rewards for everything it does for customers: by referrals, word of mouth, loyalty—the payment is there. *The judicious evaluation*: How much do you know about your customers? Do you know *why* they buy from you, *what* they buy from you, *when* they buy from you, and *how* they buy from you? Do you know in depth, in detail?

Technology has made it possible for direct marketers to separate their customer file into interrelated, subpopulation groups. The result of this subgrouping allows the development of marketing decision systems. The number of attributes which can be fed into such a system is almost infinite. With mathematical regression applications, it is possible to define and redefine segments, to establish the value of a customer, to predict sales, and to enhance new product development, which is a natural extension of most businesses.

Depending on what you know, you can then accept the challenge that leads to a return on investment. *The challenge*: to match products, messages, and offers to the customer's buying preferences and to mail more frequently and more productively to smaller groups. The *return on investment*: greater from the customer file because the sales cost is proportionately lower when compared to the cost of acquiring a new customer. But equally important, this customer profile will establish cost-effective direction for replacement needs—*new customers*.

Marketing excellence is not a goal. It is a *process*. A constant improvement in the development of data and a constant value analysis of the information supplied can and should lead to marketing imagination.

CHAPTER 7

To Whom Are You Mailing and Why?

Today's typical mailing represents an investment of approximately $300 per thousand pieces. On a mailing of 150,000 names, the total bill is *$45,000*; on 1 million names, *$300,000*; on 5 million names, *$1,500,000*; on 10 million names, *$3 million*. For that kind of money, you don't scatter-shoot. You try to predetermine.

MARKETS

A *market* is a population group, an industry, a geographical unit; it is an audience with the authority, ability, and propensity to buy certain products and services. *Market research* is collecting and analyzing data about consumer preferences, purchasing power, and needs. And the traditional backbone of market research is *demography*.

The mass marketer who advertises on TV is trying to reach the demographic group most likely to buy the maximum quantity of detergent, toothpaste, fast food, appliances, or clothing. The mass marketer hopes the ads are placed around programs which appear to deliver the audience. For example, beer commercials are usually seen on sports programs, while detergents are usually seen on daytime soap operas and game shows.

Any product's *market potential* is the total number of users of the product category, e.g., for toothpaste, the market potential is everyone with teeth. *Sales potential,* though, is the *share* of that total market the product can reasonably hope to capture. We research the market (toothpaste users) to establish how many people (or what percentage) can be persuaded to use *our* product rather than that of the competition.

Whether this is the correct approach is open to question in a dynamically moving society. Analyzing and defining our potential customers are what marketing is all about, whether we're selling as a business to consumers or as a business to other businesses. It can be done effectively only if we keep on top of the changes and trends that influence the marketplace.

As mentioned, demographics are the traditional approach: We "profile" our potential customers in terms of sex, age, marital status, income, family size, education, home ownership, and so forth, perhaps even how long the customers or prospects have lived where they live (length of residence) and in what kind of home (single-family dwelling unit) and what car (station wagon, Rolls Royce) they drive. We then try to expand our market based on the resulting statistical determinations, which in direct marketing would be by community, Zip code, carrier route, or other geographical measurement unit, and which in space and TV would be by "audience characteristics" of the publication and programs.

With mathematical techniques we can often determine the special combination of demographic factors to be found in our ideal customer. The potential universe is then calculated by the number of such profiles found in the demographic makeup of the entire country. Product development itself usually starts with this profile: determining that a profitable market exists and can be reached and sold on a cost-effective basis.

But there is a flaw in pure demographic market research. It *has* to presume that people within specific age, gender, or income categories or who live in specific neighborhoods are essentially homogeneous and that they have aspirations and lifestyles in common. This used to be a reasonable assumption, and certain mass marketers can still profitably use demographics as a type of "negative-exclusion" device.

Some products are demographically self-defining, e.g., acne treatments, disposable diapers, Jordache jeans, toys, and denture cleaners. But most are not.

Today, however, psychographics is the basis for *demassification*. It is the *humanizing* element which can't be ignored. Today is the age of multiple options—how we live, what we like, and what we care about may be very different from our near and perhaps not-so-dear neighbors and quite unlike our demographic equals.

We can't afford to forget that, increasingly, psychographics and related societal trends have come to influence demographics themselves. The trend toward exercise and health awareness as an influence on life expectancy has changed eating habits and recreational activities. It is no longer safe to assume that only high-income people play tennis or jog or are diet conscious. Technology and changing employment patterns that dictate whether we'll live in a few big cities or a lot of small ones impact geographical population distribution. Energy and ecology may reverse the trends that technology started, and so on.

Societal forces have "detached" the connective tissue that used to exist between demography and behavior. All advertisers have had to face the realism that the days of the one huge amorphous market are over. Whether you're the head of General Motors or a kid with a pitcher of lemonade to sell, you've got to know your market.

RESEARCH

While general market research is an essential ingredient in planning for direct marketing companies, it is not a panacea. Focus groups and other market research techniques are geared toward a general assessment of a particular product or service within consumer or business groups. Unfortunately, many direct marketers have paid a price for assuming that a high level of consumer acceptance resulting from this type of research is transferable to direct mail. (In actuality, these results are beneficial in product evaluation and pricing.)

For example, a major airline conducted focus groups and telephone and mail surveys and statistically projected 2 million frequent business travelers in the United States. Based on this substantial universe, the airline decided to use direct mail to promote a new travel service to this audience. At some late stage in the scenario, a list broker was brought into the picture and gave out the bad news that precise lists of frequent business travelers did not exist. There were some airline passenger lists available, but they would not be rented to this airline for competitive reasons. However, this market can be reached indirectly by inference.

A high frequency of travel can be inferred by a person's lifestyle, occupational level, and/or type of company. Sales directors for major corporations travel frequently, as do public relations executives, advertising agency executives, overseas branch managers of U.S.-based companies, to name just a few list considerations. In this specific instance, the inability to access a defined market with precision required that marketing and creative strategies be revised at the last minute which resulted in impacting the budget. How much simpler and less costly it would have been if the planning had addressed the importance of the list market.

Even with the vast number of lists available, you must understand that markets and lists are not always interrelated. Market research may precisely identify the market, but specific lists related to the particular market do not always exist.

THE COSMOS OF LISTS

In the cosmos of lists today we're confronted with thousands and thousands of them. The *challenge* for us, then, is the number of lists available, and the *opportunity* is the *variety* of the lists. This variety enables mailers to aim their products at targeted markets.

The optimum situation would be to test only those lists which prove responsive. The reality is that this is not possible. Traditionally you test mail a statistically significant sample before you mail a list. Given the sheer number of possibilities, selecting which lists to test becomes a problem in itself. List information is not linear; there are a multitude of reasoning factors which must be used.

If we keep in mind that consumer attitudes, values, and lifestyles are changing, then we must be more concerned with attitudes and preferences which dictate what the consumer will spend and for what. This is psychographic detailing. And marketing in the future will require evaluation and access on this basis.

Newcomers to direct mail will frequently talk about *a* list, one which they intend to compile themselves or find. However, it is rare that one list will do the job.

In most instances, the "prospect" definition must come from the market audit of the customer file. The more you know about your customers, the more directed the test list selection. A customer file which has been segmented to effectively create customer portraits provides a directional qualifier in the selection of lists to test. Actually, most companies initially will test new products and services on the house files to determine acceptance—and rightfully so. The success of a new product frequently will depend on the responsiveness of the house file.

The rental lists' affinity to the customer profile or defined market is quite important. Through years of experience you have found that certain types of lists work better than others. For example, publications like *Changing Times* and *Money Magazine,* which offer in-depth advice on financial and money management, find their prospects primarily among people who have expressed an interest in money management, self-improvement, career improvement, financial planning, investments, etc. Lists that fall into these categories effectively prove more responsive than other lists not so interest-defined. However, the market can be intelligently expanded by using lists based on income, occupational level, and education, such as subscribers to personal computing publications. The profiling suggests an upwardly mobile prospect with a high level of education, interest, and income. According to information supplied by various list owners in this market, about 90 percent are college-educated (many with postgraduate degrees); over 50 percent earn more than $35,000 per year; and the average age is about 38. Considering these characteristics, it is easy to conclude that they would be prospects for financial services and a variety of informational products.

If there is no internal file, planning takes on a new dimension. It is obvious then that most companies need to accumulate and evaluate information relative to the product: competition, need, and market definition. This research will guide the allocation of the dollars to determine not only how to sell but to whom and at what price.

At this point, let's say that you have already determined your marketing objectives, analyzed the strong points of your product or service, identified the competition, defined your potential customer, and developed a budget and a marketing strategy responsive to your total objectives. You decide that direct mail is the way to go. What's the next step?

THE LIST BROKER

In direct mail, the services of a recognized list broker is a must. These professionals have acquired invaluable information over years of contact with a vast variety of direct mail offers which can be applied to list availability.

With the introduction of any new product, the initial direct mail test must answer many interdisciplinary questions (price, offer, etc.), but the test *must* answer one important question. Are there lists available?

One of the problems that frequently surfaces in a new venture is *focus*—both editorially and promotionally. So often this is not predetermined, and it affects all the building blocks of direct mail. Let's look at a case in point: an "executive study system." This product was described as a home-study course for executive education geared to the development of skills required to (a) be a more effective manager and (b) assume a management-level position. In essence, it was a course to further career objectives.

The list consultant who was brought in presented a list review which represented distinctive segments which appear to be reasonably separate in definition but actually do suggest an interactive relationship (Chart 7.1).

Chart 7.1 List Market Review,
Executive Education

List Category	Universe
Seminar attendees and courses	2,239,000
Administrative management	2,434,000
Personnel training	795,000
Sales and marketing management	654,000
Small business	1,267,000
EDP, computer management, data processing	751,000
Buyers of business supplies	1,949,000
Business books and services	5,861,000
Total universe	15,950,000*

*The duplication factor will be quite high, possibly 15 to 20 percent. This potential universe should be adjusted accordingly.

However, in reading the initial promotional copy, the list review was not relevant. It was geared to top management: (1) a good deal of top management time is spent in reacting to crisis situations; (2) the causes of operational problems are not always obvious; (3) learn the analytical tools essential for disciplined decision making. In addition, there was an appeal to personnel directors: How do you, as a personnel director, recognize the highly motivated employee?

These points are made to highlight two approaches in the copy to different executive-level markets and not at all geared to middle management which, on the surface, appeared to be the market. How is it possible to select 10 test lists to determine the potential of this offer? What is required is a decision on which specific interest area to test initially and so slant the promotion. If the appeal will be to training directors and personnel management, there is a clear target. However, if the first book to be featured is *Fundamentals of Finance* or *Management of Small Business,* then the list selection and promotional criteria change.

After a thorough assessment of the copy versus the list market, a decision was made to segment and combine the books and promote each market-defined combination of books to the appropriate market (i.e., the personnel books to the personnel training category and selection by this subject within the administrative management category).

In a situation such as this, without recognizing the necessity to segment the editorial and the marketing strategies into subsets, the list selection and creative menu would not have fallen into place, and any possible early success might have resulted in ultimate failure, or early failure could have resulted in dropping the project entirely.

Never ignore the relationship between product, copy, and lists. The relationship of the list to the copy and to the product is of utmost importance.

Every action triggers a reaction. An idea is only a good idea if you take the trouble to implement it with careful and skilled management and in-depth analysis. The initial test should be considered research and development (R&D), and, unlike conventional research, some of the expense is offset by the orders received. The bottom line is *what you learn from the initial test for decision making.* That's the purpose of testing. With directional analysis there is the opportunity to come up with a positive assessment of what, on the surface, might appear to be a negative activity.

SOME BASICS FOR REVIEWING LIST SUGGESTIONS

Initial preconceptions about target markets are sometimes inaccurate, which is why an extension beyond the perceived primary market makes good business sense. To do this, it is advisable to request a complete overview of list possibilities based on:

1. A definition of the characteristics of the perceived or researched primary market and a definition of which list categories most nearly parallel this market
2. An appraisal of whether or not secondary and tertiary list markets can be identified through affinity relationship
3. Selection criteria (For example, if income, gender, age, and geography are necessary selection criteria for the product or service being offered, does the list recommendation reflect these factors?)
4. Universe potential

If these qualifications are carefully documented in the list recommendation, you should have a straightforward answer about the potential market.

SYSTEMATIC APPROACH

Let's look at the process with the magazine *Art and Artifacts.* This publication had been distributed through other channels, and direct mail had not previously been attempted. So, while this can be considered as a start-up situation for our purposes, the magazine was already being published. In a start-up situation the list recommendation submitted by the list consultant should provide an overview of the potential universe in order to ascertain that a reachable market does exist.

Preliminary research defined the market as: upwardly mobile people with above-average education and income and a demonstrated interest in art, antiques, and collectibles. The subscription price was $18 per year. (*Note:* There will be price and copy tests, but the emphasis here is on lists.)

You will note the cell organization in the overview in Chart 7.2. There is a purpose for this. *Cell 1* includes the list categories which appear right on target. *Cell 2* represents prospects who can be considered based on certain affinity factors. In some instances this does overshadow demographics. *Cell 3* reflects a different market by inference based on demographic and/or psychographic characteristics.

The question of how large a list testing program should be has no universal answer that will meet every financial situation. In a start-up situation, the test size should be sufficient to yield the data required to

**Chart 7.2   *Art and Artifacts:*
Overview of List Markets**

List Category	No. of Lists	Universe (000)
Cell 1		
Art, antiques, collectibles	31	2,995
Cultural books and magazines	31	5,232
Cultural arts	7	485
Subtotal	69	8,712
Cell 2		
Upscale gifts and decorating items	24	2,088
Photography	5	969
Regional publications	20	2,732
Subtotal	49	5,789
Cell 3		
Luxury foods, home entertainment	16	3,316
Affluent, upscale lifestyle	8	843
Miscellaneous (credit cards)	5	1,732
Subtotal	29	5,891
Total	147	20,392*

*Reduced by 25 percent due to duplication factor.

project, with a high degree of accuracy, whether the successive steps in the overall plan can be met, in other words, enabling a "go" or "no-go" decision.

Incidentally, in an ongoing situation, it is advisable to allocate 10 percent of the total quantity in each campaign to list testing. This will help avoid the problem of "list saturation." With the vast number of lists, a methodology can be developed to expand the universe so you don't run out of names.

Based on the dollar commitment developed by the *Art and Artifacts* marketing and financial team, a test quantity of 150,000 was established. This now posed the question of what to do on a test mailing of 150,000. Are we better off testing 30 lists with 5000, or should we test 15 lists with 10,000? This decision depends on the growth pattern established in the original strategic plan. On this magazine the decision was to go with the 30 lists because the objective was to find out if a subscription market existed for this magazine (Chart 7.3). You will note that while the schedule is concentrated in the more targeted categories, others were explored with an eye toward market evaluation and expansion.

Chart 7.3 Structure of List Test Schedule

Cell 1	Universe	Quantity	No. of Lists
Art, antiques, collectibles	1,215,600	45,000	9
Cultural books and magazines	876,900	25,000	5
Cultural arts	245,000	10,000	2
Subtotal	2,337,500	80,000	16
Cell 2			
Upscale gifts and decorating items	383,000	20,000	4
Photography	150,000	5,000	1
Regional publications	267,000	10,000	2
Subtotal	800,000	35,000	7
Cell 3			
Luxury foods and gifts	1,871,900	25,000	5
Affluent market	185,000	5,000	1
Miscellaneous (credit cards)	125,000	5,000	1
Subtotal	2,181,900	35,000	7
Total	5,319,400	150,000	30

Chart 7.4 Summary of Mailing Results: Art and Artifacts

1. Actual mail quantity	150,615
2. Number of orders	3,269
3. Percent response	2.17
4. Package cost per thousand	$225.00
5. List cost per thousand	$50.21
6. Total cost	$41,451.00
7. Total cost per thousand	$275.21
8. Gross cost per subscriber	$12.68
9. Percent credit	90.4
10. Percent bad pay	33.16
11. Net subscribers	2,289
12. Net percent response	1.52
13. Net cost per subscriber	$18.11
14. Total revenue (on net)	$45,711.00
15. Net revenue (total revenue minus total cost)	$4,260.00
16. Net revenue per subscriber	$1.86

MOMENT OF TRUTH

The moment of truth: The mailing results are available. Chart 7.4 gives a summary of the results.

How were these figures developed? Here are the clues:

1. **Actual mail quantity.** From the postal receipt received at the post office by the mailing service (letter shop).
2. **Number of orders.** These numbers are generated through the order entry system the company uses.
3. **Percent response.** Based on the number of orders divided by the mail quantity:

$$\frac{3,269}{150,615} = 2.17 \text{ percent}$$

4. **Cost per thousand.** This is the actual cost which includes: promotion package, merge/purge costs, and letter shop costs to insert, sort, and mail including postage.
5. **List cost per thousand.** Based on actual list rental costs.
6. **Total cost for this promotion.** Actual costs are derived from invoices received for services plus postage.
7. **Total cost per thousand.** This is arrived at by taking the total cost divided by the mail quantity:

$$\frac{\$41,451}{150,615} = \$275.21/M$$

$$150,615 \times 275.21/M = \$41,451$$

8. **Gross cost per subscriber.** The total cost ($41,451) divided by the number of orders (3269) equals $12.68.

9. **Percent credit.** Since the offer included a bill-me option, this factor is input at order entry for billing purposes. In this case, 90.4 percent of the orders requested credit.

10. **Percent bad pay.** The 33.16 percent figure is developed from the billing cycle. This figure represents customers or prospects who did not pay.

11. **Net subscribers.** This figure represents the final number of paid subscribers.

$$3269 \text{ gross orders} \times 90.4 = 2955 \text{ credit orders}$$
$$3269 - 2955 \text{ credit orders} = 314 \text{ cash orders}$$

Of the 2955 credit orders, 33.16 percent did not pay:

$$2955 \times 33.16 \text{ percent} = 980$$

So, if we take 2955 credit orders minus the 980 who did not pay and add the cash orders, we get net orders of 2289.

$$2955 - 980 + 314 = 2289$$

12. **Net percent response.**

$$\frac{2,289}{150,615} = 1.52$$

13. **Net cost per subscriber.**

$$\frac{\$41,451}{2,289} = \$18.11$$

14. **Total revenue (on net)**

$$2289 \times 19.97 = \$45,711$$

15. **Net revenue (total revenue minus total cost)**

$$\$45,711 - \$41,451 = \$4,260$$

16. **Net revenue per subscriber.**

$$\frac{\$4260 \text{ net revenue}}{2289 \text{ net orders}} = \$1.86$$

It is important to understand that the same factors used in the summary also were applied on a *list-by-list* basis within each category. To demonstrate, though, that averages can sometimes be misleading, refer to Chart 7.5, which details the first category: art, antiques, and collectibles. The average net revenue is $2.04; the average net percent response is 1.54. On an individual list basis, net revenue runs from a negative $19.88 to a positive $8.49, and net percent response runs from a low of 0.68 to a high of 2.40. *And* look at list 8 which produced the highest upfront response but was demolished by the bad-pay factor: almost twice the average.

In analyzing by categories, it is sounder, particularly in the initial stages (and especially on a test with equal list quantities) to use the number of lists tested within each category in order to develop the success ratio (Chart 7.6).

This analysis was correlated to the cells of the test spectrum. In addition, you will observe that the test configuration does emphasize the relative importance of the perceived primary market but also affords the opportunity to examine and thus expand the potential universe which was the objective of this test.

Analysis by list categorization is not an absolute science. Some lists in the same category are not responsive for an infinite number of reasons. But this process is directional. To further the fact-finding process, examine the good-responding versus the poor-responding lists based on criteria such as recency, frequency, unit of sale, source of names, geography, gender, demographics, and psychographics. This could point to the underlying ingredients that make a list work and would contribute to a list selection system similar to ADI (area of dominant influence) research measurement. In other words, this analysis could reveal which DDIs (discriminants of dominant influence) appear to impact most heavily on response.

THE CONTINUATION MAILING: FROM STRATEGY TO STRUCTURE

In the case of *Art and Artifacts*, the initial test mailing approached the level of financial success necessary to continue. It was decided to do another mailing in October 1984.

As you will note in Chart 7.7, the continuation mailing was structured along the cell configuration. Since the risk is obviously less in the upper two cells, the bulk of the list testing was so concentrated. The quantity allocated to list tests is a bit high, but the growth objectives established by the management team made it essential to explore as many new lists as possible. Normally, 10 percent of the total mail quantity is recommended for list testing.

Chart 7.5 Art and Artifacts Test Mailing, April 1984 (List Category: Art, Antiques, and Collectibles)

List	Mail Qty.	No. of Orders	% Response	Pkg. CPM	List CPM	Total CPM	CPO	% Credit	% Bad Pay	Net Orders	Net % Response	Net CPO	Total Cost	Total Revenue	Net Revenue	Net Revenue per Subscriptions
1	5,008	155	3.10	$225	$45	$270	$8.72	88.0	58.8	75	1.50	$18.03	$1,352	$1,498	$ 146	$1.94
2	5,004	145	2.90	225	55	280	9.66	91.0	41.7	90	1.80	15.57	1,401	1,797	396	4.40
3	5,050	152	3.00	225	50	275	9.14	89.0	23.0	121	2.40	11.48	1,389	2,416	1,027	8.49
4	4,999	140	2.80	225	55	280	10.00	82.0	21.7	115	2.30	12.17	1,400	2,297	897	7.80
5	5,010	60	1.20	225	45	270	22.55	94.0	35.2	40	0.80	33.82	1,353	799	(554)	(13.85)
6	5,300	154	2.91	225	55	280	9.64	91.0	60.7	69	1.30	21.51	1,484	1,378	(106)	(1.54)
7	5,080	152	2.99	225	60	285	9.53	85.0	26.0	118	2.32	12.27	1,448	2,356	908	7.70
8	5,020	156	3.11	225	45	270	8.69	92.0	84.7	34	0.68	39.85	1,355	679	(676)	(19.88)
9	5,010	55	1.10	225	45	270	24.60	96.0	33.4	37	0.74	36.56	1,353	739	(614)	(16.59)
Subtotal:	45,481	1169	2.57	$225	$50.61	$275.61	$10.72	89.0	45.2	699	1.54	17.93	$12,535	$13,959	$1,424	$2.04

**Chart 7.6   Success Factor Analysis
by Cell Configuration**

Cell 1	No. of Lists	No. of Successes*	Percent Success
Arts, antiques, collectibles	9	5	55.6
Cultural reading	5	5	100.0
Cultural arts	2	1	50.0
Subtotal	16	11	68.8
Cell 2			
Upscale merchandise	4	1	25.0
Photography	1	1	100.0
Regional magazines	2	2	100.0
Subtotal	7	4	57.1
Cell 3			
Luxury foods and gifts	5	2	40.0
Affluent market	1	1	100.0
Miscellaneous (credit cards)	1	—	—
Subtotal	7	3	42.9
Total	30	18	60.0

*Based on net revenue per subscriber

The selection criteria on the lists previously used were to include in the plan any list that had produced a positive net revenue per subscriber and a retest of any list with a negative net revenue under $2. This would not necessarily be the decision criteria in every case. For example, gross response might be used if "numbers" are important and the conversion factor is good.

The assumptions used to project the mailing were: 10 percent reduction on response for test to retest; an overall 5 percent quantity reduction from merge/purge; and 3 percent increase in response for seasonality. Please bear in mind that these were applied on a list-by-list basis using previous response as the starting point.

FRAMEWORK FOR PLANNING

Basically, previous results must be quantified in order to forecast as accurately as possible what might happen on the next campaign. There

Chart 7.7 Overall Summary, Projected Mail Plan

	Gross Qty.	Net Qty.	% Response	Gross Subscriptions	List CPM	Total CPM	Total Cost	CPO	% Credit	% Bad Pay	Net Orders	Net % Response	Net CPO	Total Revenue	Net Revenue	Net Revenue per Subscription
Cell 1																
Art, antiques, collectibles	275,000	261,250	2.74	7,154	$55.98	$280.98	$ 73,406	$10.26	87.4	37.2	4,829	1.85	$15.20	$ 96,435	$23,029	$4.77
Cultural reading	250,000	237,500	2.80	6,650	57.89	282.89	67,186	10.10	90.0	27.0	5,034	2.12	13.35	100,529	33,343	6.62
Cultural arts	50,000	47,500	2.59	1,230	52.63	277.63	13,187	10.72	89.0	28.0	923	1.94	14.29	18,432	$ 5,245	$5.68
List tests	90,000	85,500	2.20	1,881	52.63	277.63	23,737	12.62	90.0	35.0	1,288	1.51	18.43	25,721	1,984	1.54
Total cell 1	665,000	631,750	2.68	16,915	$55.99	$280.99	$177,516	$10.50	88.8	32.2	12,074	1.91	$14.70	$241,117	$63,601	$5.27
Cell 2																
Upscale merchandise	25,000	23,750	1.76	418	$52.63	$277.63	$ 6,594	$15.78	89.0	30.0	306	1.29	$21.55	$ 6,111	($ 483)	($1.58)
Photography	50,000	47,500	2.60	1,235	47.37	272.37	12,938	10.48	87.5	26.4	950	2.00	13.62	18,972	6,034	6.35
Regional magazines	100,000	95,000	2.46	2,337	57.89	282.89	26,875	11.50	92.1	26.5	1,767	1.86	15.21	35,287	8,412	4.76
List tests	40,000	38,000	1.75	665	52.63	277.63	10,550	15.86	90.0	27.0	503	1.32	20.97	10,045	(505)	(1.00)
Total cell 2	215,000	204,250	2.28	4,655	$53.86	$278.86	$56,957	$12.24	90.3	26.9	3,526	1.73	$16.15	$70,415	$13,458	$3.82
Cell 3																
Luxury foods	50,000	47,500	2.13	1,012	$52.63	$277.63	$13,187	$13.03	90.2	24.0	793	1.67	$16.63	$15,836	$2,649	$3.34
Affluent market	50,000	47,500	2.21	1,050	63.16	288.16	13,688	13.04	88.7	25.5	813	1.71	16.84	16,235	2,547	3.13
Miscellaneous (credit card)	—	—	—	—	—	—	—	—	—	—	—	—	—	—	—	—
List tests	20,000	19,000	1.70	323	57.89	282.89	5,375	16.64	90.0	25.0	250	1.32	21.50	4,993	(382)	(1.53)
Total cell 3	120,000	114,000	2.09	2,385	$57.89	$282.89	$32,250	$13.52	89.5	24.8	1,856	1.63	$17.38	$37,064	$4,814	$2.59
Total continuations	850,000	807,500	2.61	21,086	$56.19	$281.19	$227,061	$10.77	89.0	30.2	15,415	1.91	$14.73	$307,837	$80,776	$5.24
Total list tests	150,000	142,500	2.01	2,869	53.33	278.33	39,662	13.82	90.0	32.1	2,041	1.43	19.43	40,759	1,097	0.54
Grand total	1,000,000	950,000	2.52	23,955	$55.76	$280.76	$266,723	$11.13	89.2	30.4	17,456	1.84	$15.28	$348,596	$81,873	$4.69

are, however, decision influencers that are hard to qualify except after the fact, for example, the external environment: the economy, weather, or dramatic events. Most direct mail managers recognize the impact of external events on prediction but also are aware that all are not in our sphere of influence, particularly when most direct mail campaigns are, of necessity, planned 3 to 4 months before the actual mail date.

What can be controlled is the ability to effectively manage information—a key resource—which depends on the constant enhancement of the quality of the data collected.

Predictions are difficult at best; "overpromise" can be a disaster. Management tends to be more impressed by a plan which anticipates a drop-off for sound reasons rather than a plan which needs to be completely justified after the fact.

In direct mail there is an impressive arena for testing and, through proper analysis, *discovery*. An experiment is never a failure if you learn something from it. It is essential that all variables be identified, controlled, and statistically measured on a continuing basis because the primary, indeed the only, objective of testing is to gain knowledge—the knowledge that is the framework for planning.

Information: A Mirror to the Future

When direct mail managers express disappointment with the mail campaign, they're actually revealing that the campaign did not meet their projections. But the question is, what did they project? What did they expect? And on what basis? And was the mail plan projected from previous experience? Let's see what might have happened.

Effective scheduling is more than meeting deadlines. Making the right decisions requires the right data. Direct mail, to be successful, must give weight to all its parts: product, copy, offer, package, pricing, fulfillment, markets, costs, and lists. Under this concept all the players can be positioned as co-architects. Think of the mailing plan as an architectural arrangement of building blocks involving design, structure, examination, and evaluation—a system considered from the point of view of the whole rather than of any single part. However, most direct mail practitioners concede that the list scores a high value in this mix. Yet frequently the list rates a backseat in the planning process.

One point must be emphasized. In the past, there were some direct mail practitioners who had only a very superficial knowledge of the financial dynamics of direct mail; and some financial executives had almost no understanding of the medium. This combination did have a negative effect on profits and in some instances the company's ability to stay in business. Times have changed. Accountability is the name of our game. Rich dividends can accrue if close attention is given to the financial details of assembling a mailing plan. It is essential to allocate dollars for maximum return, and to do that requires actionable information, not volumes of data.

While planning is the essential ingredient in any business, in direct mail—a complex activity—it is critical. This complexity is also a strength because many of the variables can be identified and mathematically measured. The mail plan is the process of putting into numerical terms the expected results of that mailing. It is the instrument that must be used to evaluate actual results. It is a thread analysis with information checkpoints: history on lists, offers, mail date, price, and assumptions. If the thread is broken, you will find that the misplaced decimal point will end up where it can do the most damage.

In developing a mail plan, where the outcome has a degree of uncertainty, success lies not in avoiding risk but in holding it within acceptable limits. Actually, disciplined "risk taking" which is based on a thorough analysis of previous experience can be very rewarding. Financial planners call it the "risk-reward ratio." Any investment program (and in our terms the mail plan) does depend on the amount of investment money available. This helps to fix the kind of risks you can afford to take as well as quantifying the stake if you lose. But the quantitative should not ignore the qualitative. So, determine your objectives and analyze the resources needed to achieve them—realistically.

Look at the macro picture of the direct mail campaign as a series of micro adventures (tests). The end product will be information—the market research necessary for your next mail campaign. The objective is to bring in the most customers, at the lowest cost, with the most revenue. Sometimes, however, objectives are colored by wishful thinking. If you're powered by hope, fired by hunch, and guided by intuition, fine. However, calculated risks can frequently be more productive than "a point of view." Always remember that the quantitative should not ignore the qualitative and vice versa.

MAKING THE RIGHT DECISION
REQUIRES THE RIGHT DATA

Greater productivity in direct mail is a function of gathering, understanding, and using information. It's axiomatic, too, that if we don't understand where we've been, it's very hard to figure out where we're going. Without careful attention to the meaning of the numbers, we have no basis for planning the next move and beyond.

Where do we start? With record keeping. Not miles and piles of computer printouts but disciplined, comprehensive, and systematic record keeping. Once the integrity of your system has been established, the data collection function (manual or computerized) should not be difficult to follow.

Without complete and permanent records, decisions can be haphazard and costly. For example, in one case an extensive and expensive test was beautifully set up and conducted. Results were clear and definitive. Yet, through sloppy record keeping and change in personnel, the final results were misinterpreted, and a completely wrong decision followed.

SITUATION ANALYSIS

In this perspective, consider the mail plan analagous to strategic planning. In a broad simplistic sense, strategic planning is a research operation, a process of gathering facts about your business and asking questions, in other words, developing decision criteria. From the preliminary answers you begin to identify the elements that will shape your strategic plan, in this case your direct mail campaign.

In reviewing the previous plan (whether results were good or bad), what did you learn? What matters in a cause-and-effect analysis is not a subjective defense of the plan but an objective and thoughtful evaluation. What influences can be specifically measured which will assist in positioning the assumptions for the next campaign? For example:

1. Were there too many tests which affected overall results? What would have been the outcome had these tests been excluded?
2. Were the tests significant (as in *breakthrough*) or just minor variations on an old theme?
3. What influences can be measured specifically? For example, were the assumptions used in developing the plan realistic? Sometimes those ideas that feel so rich and full in our heads become rather thin and watery when quantified.
4. Were there too many list tests or not enough? Were new markets tested?
5. Were the house files used to the fullest extent possible? If so, are they holding up or falling down in response? Are there additional segmentation techniques which can be supplied?
6. Were financial resources allocated on the basis of how much you are willing to invest in new-customer acquisition versus how much you are

willing to invest in retaining present customers? For example, would it be more cost-effective for a magazine or book or record club to offer a premium or any other incentive to retain a subscriber rather than invest in new-customer acquisition?

These are just a sprinkling of the specifics which can be studied in a situation analysis. It is essential to develop methods of comparing actual performance to planned objectives, identifying trends, and taking corrective actions when needed. Reports should highlight key variances which need to be investigated. The unprecedented availability of information has made *data selection* just as critical as the data itself. Sometimes decisions are difficult to make because either data does not exist or it exists in such volume that critical facts are lost in the mass.

PORTFOLIO ANALYSIS

Whether or not you subscribe to the portfolio analysis concept in strategic planning, this does seem to be the heuristic approach here. In the direct mail environment, the portfolio does consist of lists. And with lists we are talking about experimentation (trial and error). Any self-educating techniques that can be employed to improve list selection and usage will pay off handsomely.

The list-by-list history is fundamental to the information gathering process. Whether manual or electronic, the planning process begins with the list record in detail, with each list representing a medium, not an amalgam of media. Each list must be detailed by the variables needed to evaluate the performance. Individual lists are exactly that.

All of this may appear to be academic; every company has that list record. In reality, every company does *not*. Most companies have the final mailing report on a campaign-by-campaign basis, and lists are obviously included. But the list-by-list performance record covering all the campaigns in which the list was used is not always in place.

HARD FACTS AND CRISP ANALYSIS

To estimate the results of a mail plan, certain variables must be identified, and assumptions relative to the effect of the variables must be used in the projections. This is analogous to economic advisors who look at leading indicators (and sometimes reach different conclusions). It's a question of interpretation and the weight given to certain factors. For example, if the total quantity mailed was and will be governed by the need to meet a rate base rather than the quantity which could be mailed at a break-even level, a high weight must be given to this objective and the financial implications.

Here are the variables which, from experience, have a decided impact on results:

Seasonality

Years of study and evaluation seem to show that certain categories of products sold by direct mail have certain time periods of the year in which the climate is better than others. Some are obvious, for example, fall fashion catalogs in July and August or Christmas catalogs in the fall. In certain parts of the country, late winter to early spring are better for gardening products. In other parts of the country, gardening products can be sold practically throughout the year. Most, though, are not so obvious.

The seasonality study in Appendix 8A can be directional, but each company should determine, through controlled testing, which months or seasons are best for their product or service. This can be done on a monthly basis by mailing the same offer at the same time every month to comparable but different names from the same list. Then, the company can carefully tabulate the results.

Monthly change-of-address names are best for this type of test, the reason being that they are of comparable quality each month. They're better than hotlines for this purpose. Hotline names may be secured from different sources, thus introducing a variable. The direct mail names generated one month could be stronger than the space- or TV-sold names you get in subsequent months. But a change of address from July should react similarly to a change of address from August because there should, on average, be no source bias.

With a disciplined and continuing seasonality test, you can determine with some degree of certainty that March is 10 percent better than May but 10 percent worse than January and so on. This increase or decrease can be applied to individual lists in the campaign depending upon the seasonal variance between the month the list was last used versus the month for which you are projecting.

Price Test

Testing price is easier to quantify than seasonality. If the new price was tested, you should have a good idea of the impact on results. For example, you sold your book at $14.95 in January but tested $17.95 on lists used in the hotline mailing. Response dropped by 10 percent on the

$17.95 price; nevertheless, this price will be used in the fall mailing. In forecasting response, you must differentiate between lists that have already seen the higher price and those that haven't. The decrease should be applied only to those lists which were not included in the original price test. This lends itself to the "income per thousand names mailed" described in Chapter 5 (see Chart 5.5).

In addition, look at the back end. In one recent situation where a price test was conducted, the new price depressed initial response and increased the cost per order. However, when the response was tracked through conversions, conversions were up by 11 percent resulting in a substantial increase in net revenues per converted order. In this case, if only front-end response had been analyzed, the lower price would have prevailed.

Package

Very frequently a new package is tested in a relatively small quantity (25,000). If the new package produced a 50 percent lift on a test panel, it would be unwise to apply this substantial increase over an entire continuation volume. From experience a more conservative approach is indicated. A 20 percent or 25 percent increase might be more reasonable, and the cost of the package should be adjusted to reflect the economies of scale. This is necessary in order to come up with the correct cost per order (Chart 8.1). *Another example:* The fact that a mailing pulled 1.5 percent in December and a new package test gave a 20 percent lift cannot be extrapolated to mean that, for the July mailing, a 1.8 percent can be expected. That's a simplistic approach to a fairly complex problem.

Test To Retest To Continuation

If a statistically valid sampling is provided on a test, the results on a large run should be consistent within a standard deviation factor. In actual practice, however, it is rare that the larger quantity runs parallel to the test results. Occasionally the drop-off can be so great as to be almost disastrous. There are many reasons why this can happen and here are a few:

1. The test was not a true representative sampling of the list. This does affect the continuation because test results are meaningful only if they are totally representative of the continuation. This can be accomplished only by a true random or Nth-name selection for the continuation portion (except if the entire balance of a list is used). Any procedural deviation will tend to invalidate the test.

2. There was a long time lag between the test and the follow-up. The composition of the list could have changed due to offers, source, etc. On a compiled list which is not updated on a regular basis, the list could have a high degree of undeliverables. Also the timing between tests and continuation introduces a factor of change from the external situation that existed at the time of the test. As we all know, political polls are always prefaced with the statement "If the election were held today."

3. The test was mailed in a good season, and the run, in a poor season. Attempts must be made to incorporate the seasonality factors into projections. Seasonality is selective; the best season for one product is not necessarily the best for a different product. Therefore, "tailor-made" seasonality trends will prove more successful.

4. The test was small (5000), and the continuation quantity was 100,000. The test quantity may have been insufficient to yield the information needed to cope with the elements of risk involved in a rollout of 100,000 names (20 times the test quantity). The philosophical answer to "how big should the sample be?" is that it should be large enough to enable decisions to be made within an acceptable degree of risk, and no more; a job for the statistician.

5. There were external influences such as weather, dramatic news events, or poor economic news. Accounting for economic cycles, for example, can become especially important when there is a long period between test and continuation. Major changes in the economy sometimes occur precipitously, but this is not usual. Economic forecasts by government agencies, private organizations, and institutions are available on a continuing basis. Use those which appear suited to your operations or those in which you have some degree of confidence, and integrate some of these indicators into your predictive mode. Sometimes in-house regression analysis or other statistical techniques may yield important directions. A major business-to-business marketer was able to develop its own highly reliable "index of leading indicators" which allowed it to anticipate business cycles with a high degree of accuracy.

6. Competition may have been a factor. Intense competitive activity can be a serious problem but one which is difficult to manage. Even though list owners usually provide adequate protection against competitive products, there is a lack of real control; a mailer may not adhere to the assigned mail date and/or the postal service may have delivered the mail on a delayed basis.

It appears that it is prudent in forecasting to lower the test response on a list by 10 percent when rolling out from a 5000 or 10,000 test to a retest quantity (15,000 to 50,000), and by 15 to 20 percent if a larger slice of the list is being mailed.

Statisticians can suggest many theories as to why this might happen. The practical reality is, however, that it does happen with consistent frequency. Generally, the smaller the test, the more fluctuation you'll see on a rollout. A rollout which is more than 10 times the test quantity (except if the test response was *extremely* high) can be compared to shooting crap for high stakes.

Repeat Usage of Same Names

This factor is difficult to quantify. But it is logical to assume that the same group of names that pulled 1.9 percent in January will not pull the same response in August. A second solicitation in a 6-month period will be less productive than the first. If you can afford a 25 to 30 percent drop in response, the list could be worth repeating. However, if the list is an active one with new names being added and old names dropped, the "repeat" becomes less repetitive, and the list should hold up within a 10 to 15 percent range.

In very general terms, the smaller interest-defined, highly targeted files can be used more frequently than larger lists which are not as specific and vertical in nature.

If you have used a list three times in the last year and the third use did not meet expectations, don't give up. Try resting it for 12 months. If the list is still active, you'll be pleasantly surprised at how it will rebound.

One thought: If you use the same list or lists over and over again, try changing the envelope.

Allocation of Mail Dates in Multiproduct Companies

In a multiproduct company the allocation of mail dates to the various products can be a problem and could impact on projections and response, particularly when pretty much the same markets are covered. If you have 12 or more which mail two times per year, you face the problem of allocating mail dates in the "good" months. Since seasonality is an important ingredient in direct mail, the scheduling of mail dates may need to be measured and assigned on a formula basis.

This formula could possibly be defined by a productivity analysis of each service in terms of its past experience, future prospects, and return on investment. Is it in a growing market? Declining market? How many units have been sold? Is the sale and/or profit curve ascending or descending? The analysis should address any other considerations which apply, for example, the fact that certain products go through a life cycle that is analogous to life. First there is birth, then growth, then a period of maturity followed by decline. (Terrible thought, isn't it?)

This assessment is important because it provides a basis for allocating today's resources against tomorrow's business. It's possible that a product which is successful and has a high return on investment can continue to generate a reasonable profit even if assigned a low-priority mail date. Conversely, a product which is new and does not yet contribute to profit might need to be assigned a high-priority mailing period in order to accelerate the return on investment. In a financial sense, you're considering the risk-reward trade-off and return on investment balancing act.

It's a matter of looking at the various products and evaluating them much as you might manage a portfolio of stocks. Some should be held for current dividends, some should be actively pursued for growth, and some should be divested to free capital for more profitable investment. The allocation of resources is a complex subject. While the portfolio of stocks may not be a perfect analogy, it does convey the nuance of the intended message.

VARIABLES WHICH IMPACT COSTS

While the following variables do not impact percent response, they do impact costs and must be included in the assumptions used to structure the mail plan. These are: change in cost of the package, postage, and net-name arrangements. For example, if the previous mailing was too small to gain any cost benefit (postage) from carrier route sorting but this campaign will, this cost reduction must be addressed in the plan. Or if the package cost was based on a small quantity, then the economies of scale must be considered (see Chart 8.1, Economies of Scale).

As you will see, there is an $8 per thousand difference from top to bottom on package costs but $32 per thousand on postage.

Chart 8.1   Economies of Scale

Qty.	Pkg.	Postage*	Merge/Purge	Letter Shop	Total
300,000	$120	$124.00	$10.00	$7.50	$261.50
600,000	120	117.00	8.00	7.50	252.50
900,000 to 1,500,000	117	93.00	6.50	7.50	224.00
2,000,000 to 2,500,000	114	92.50	6.50	7.50	220.50
Over 2,500,000	112	92.00	6.50	7.50	218.00

*Based on the estimated quantity which can be presorted by five-digit Zip code and carrier route.

INCONSISTENCIES

The various inconsistencies described make the projections complicated—and sometimes frustrating. But any direct mail manager who does not acknowledge their existence is asking for trouble.

STAYING IN CONTROL

Realistically, the most important document we ever write is the business plan, budget, forecast, or whatever you call it in your company. This exercise is detailed and complex—not glamorous, but without it no company can structure a direct mail campaign. No company will ever know why a promotion failed or was successful without documentation. Here are the basic record tools:

1. **The mail plan including projections.** Lists, keys, gross quantities, net quantities, offers, etc., as described in Chapter 7 relative to the *Art and Artifacts* mail plan.
2. **Daily or weekly response reports showing not only daily or weekly response but also cumulative response.** A systematic review of this report can help establish a "rate-of-return curve." Knowing that 40 percent of the total orders were received by the third week after drop date would prove invaluable in projecting response for a subsequent campaign if final response is not available at planning time. You must be careful about using other people's data on this subject because it may not apply to you. The pattern observed for subscriptions will be different from that observed in catalogs.
3. **Final report.** The original mail plan should be adjusted to reflect actual quantities and costs. This report then is a financial report through actual net cost per order. It is also a comprehensive, multipurpose communication tool which evaluates the mailing, pointing out both good and bad points for future reference and, very important, comparing projected results versus actual. Chart 8.2, Forecast versus Actual, represents a summary for the year. Actually, each mailing was thoroughly reviewed during the year. For example, in the March mailing, a quantity of 250,000 names was used for package (150,000) and price testing (100,000). The latter depressed response by 12 percent, and the overall package tests reduced response by 2 percent.
   Keep the final report open for the back-end details such as percent bad pay, net orders, net percent response, and net CPO. It is very definitely in the "back end" that you will know whether the mailing was a success.
4. **Individual list history.** At the conclusion of each mailing, the results obtained on each list should be posted to an individual list history card

Chart 8.2 Summary: Forecast versus Actual
Investment Choice Newsletter

	Forecasted				Actual				Variance			
	Mail Qty.	Orders	Percent Response	CPO	Mail Qty.	Orders	Percent Response	CPO	Mail Qty.	Orders	Percent Response	CPO
January	1,555,520	7,871	0.51	$36.68	1,645,101	7,695	0.47	$41.27	5.7	(2.2)	(7.8)	$12.5
March	1,517,800	6,008	0.40	48.27	1,495,341	5,851	0.39	50.04	(1.5)	(2.6)	(2.5)	3.7
June	1,464,200	7,396	0.51	38.17	1,669,619	7,397	0.44	42.98	14.0	—	(13.7)	12.6
July	794,400	3,800	0.48	$41.06	586,535	2,471	0.42	$48.40	2.6	(3.4)	(12.5)	$17.8
September	787,520	3,382	0.43	46.32	845,666	3,187	0.38	50.64	7.3	(5.7)	(11.6)	9.3
October	1,500,200	6,852	0.46	40.66	1,617,248	7,095	0.44	41.82	7.8	3.5	(4.3)	2.9
Total 1984	7,619,640	35,309	0.46	$41.13	7,859,510	33,696	0.43	$44.69	3.1	4.6	(6.5)	$8.7

or to the computer list history data base. A continuing list record over a period of time (at least 2 years) and over a variety of offers can establish the efficiency of a particular list.

AFTER THE MAILING IS OVER: BACK END

The popular descriptor "back end" means persistence. It appears that, because direct mail is not purely a "front-end" business, "back end" became the popular nomenclature. Back end is where the profits are. No matter what business you're in, it is essential to know how a customer performs. To know this (front-end) response must be tracked to develop persistency (back end).

Some companies have arranged their analysis program in such a way that orders cannot be tracked in quantities of less than 50. In such instances, knowing that lists will not respond uniformly, it is essential that you test (assuming a 1 percent response) in quantities of 7500. However, if your anticipated response (based on either experience or intuitive judgment) is 2 percent, you can go with a 5000 test.

Obviously, the effective sample size for a tracking study is the number of starts—not the quantity mailed. As an example, let's take a look at the importance of payment patterns in evaluating results. In mail-order selling, one of the most productive offers is that which says, "Send no money. We'll bill you later." If charge business is accepted, collections become an integral part of the final response.

Some marketers assume an average "no-pay" figure for all lists and sometimes assume that an upper-income audience will have fewer uncollectible accounts. These assumptions can prove costly. The upper-income prospect is more discerning and may decide that the product or service is not attractive from a personal need point of view. Actually, there are lists well above and below the average so an arbitrary bad-debt factor is not only impractical but misleading (Chart 8.3).

Note that list A which had the highest gross return also had one of the lowest collection percentages. Lists C and D had approximately the same gross, but on net returns list C was definitely better. List E, a top demographic list of businessmen, had only a 68 percent collection rate. List G, with the lowest gross, had the second highest collectibility rate. Compared against gross returns, the average drop-off for all lists was 16.6 percent, but on individual lists, this percentage varied from 6.3 to 27.1 percent. The most responsive lists initially are not necessarily the best.

Ideally, all orders should be tracked by list for collectibility. If this is not possible, tracking a carefully selected sampling of orders from each list will provide the necessary indicator.

Chart 8.3 Send No Money

List	Gross Orders	No. of Charge	Percent Charge	Percent of Charge Who Paid	No. of Nonpays	Percent Nonpays	Net Orders	Percent Drop vs. Gross
A	168	84	50.0	56.0	37	44.0	131	22.0
B	144	72	50.0	87.5	9	12.5	135	6.3
C	119	60	50.4	70.0	18	30.0	101	15.1
D	118	59	50.0	45.8	32	54.2	86	27.1
E	99	50	50.5	68.0	16	32.0	83	16.2
F	90	45	50.0	61.0	18	40.0	72	20.0
G	89	45	50.6	84.4	7	15.6	82	7.9
	827	415	50.2	67.0	137	33.0	690	16.6

ANALYSIS AND MORE ANALYSIS

1. Chart 8.4 is an analysis of list usage (over a 2-year period) by category indexed by *response* and is a valuable decision identifier. This type of analysis can reveal the need for new promotional copy to appeal to a specific market or, conversely, to stop testing in that market. At a cost

Chart 8.4 Analysis of List Usage by Category, Indexed by Response

Category	Index	Qty. Mailed (000)
Cultural interest	100	2163
History	93	405
Parents and children	74	1851
Credit cards	66	1380
Outdoors, nature, conservation	64	612
Military	62	100
Boating	61	34
Health, self-improvement	57	185
Hobbies	53	236
Reading (mail interest)	53	1346
Professional, civic	51	152
General reading	47	264
Horticulture	39	344
Women's magazines	38	5
General merchandise	35	47
Compiled	34	91

Note: Cultural reading was used as the base because it represented the best category based on response.

of $300+ in the mail, testing 20 lists at 5000 each (which incidentally is the minimum test on most lists today) costs $30,000. This is too much to spend to find the one list which may work in a particular category (cost-reward again). In this example, any category indexed at over 55 was breakeven or profitable. This clearly shows which list avenues should be further penetrated.

2. Chart 8.5 is an analysis by list category over three mailings based on *net cost per order*. The percentage of total pieces mailed for each category is as follows:

Category	Percent of Total
Fashion	21.3
Shelter and home decorating	16.0
Art and antiques	17.2
	54.5
Business, finance	4.3
Regional publications	5.3
Upscale merchandise	26.1
	35.7
Gourmet items	3.0
General publications	4.1
Low-end merchandise	2.7
	9.8

**Chart 8.5   Summary by Category
Based on Net CPO**

Category	Mail Qty.	Gross Response	Percent Bad Pay	Net Response	Net CPO
Fashion	558,142	5.71	42.4	3.29	$ 5.09
Shelter and home decorating	420,264	4.50	41.3	2.64	6.84
Art and antiques	451,936	3.08	41.8	1.79	9.91
Business, finance	114,048	2.47	45.7	1.37	11.49
Regional publications	139,383	2.92	45.5	1.59	11.51
Upscale merchandise	685,529	2.98	46.3	1.60	11.53
Gourmet items	77,871	2.67	47.1	1.41	14.72
General publications	108,736	2.72	61.4	1.05	17.50
Low-end merchandise	69,559	2.50	57.2	1.07	19.60
Total	2,625,468	3.76	44.1	2.10	$ 8.50

Note that categories for fashion, shelter and home decorating, and art and antiques yielded the most acceptable net cost per order. These categories represent 54.5 percent of the total pieces mailed. On the low end, general publications, gourmet items, and low-end merchandise yielded the highest net-cost figures. Fortunately, they represent only 9.8 percent of the total mailings.

This method of associative grouping over a period of time enables the list tests to be concentrated in what appears to be the most attractive gathering of prospects.

Incidentally, this is an excellent way to structure schedules and analyze results—by list markets. It can be directional in developing affinity relationships which can assist in selecting test lists and even other media on a practical basis. This does not necessarily involve computers; small companies can do this manually because mailing volume is, relatively speaking, small.

3. Another meaningful analysis can be based on the duplication factor by list against the house file. Since most companies do merge lists to remove duplication, one facet that was subjected to scrutiny was the possible correlation between a list's duplication factor with the internal file and its success. There has always been the feeling that a correlation did exist. Chart 8.6 shows the results of one case.

You can see that the variation between the 20 percent dupe rate and under 15 percent was 31.2 percent. This result was very significant. Further analysis showed that 7 out of the 14 lists with a dupe rate of 20 percent or more pulled 3 percent or better. Only one out of eight lists

**Chart 8.6   Match Rate Analysis:
Outside Lists versus House File**

Number of lists analyzed	30
Average Dupe Factor	20%
Average Response	
Lists exceeding 20% dupe rate	2.88%
Lists with dupe rate of 15 to 19.99%	2.58%
Lists with dupe rate below 15%	1.98%
Lists over 20% dupe rate pulling 3% or better	7 out of 14 (50%)
Lists with dupe rate between 15 and 19.9% pulling 3% or better	1 out of 8 (12.5%)
Lists below 15% pulling 3% or better	0 out of 8 (0%)

with a dupe rate between 15 and 20 percent pulled 3 percent or better. None of the eight lists with a dupe rate of under 15 percent pulled 3 percent.

This study is still continuing in order to back test these findings. If confirmed with a reasonable degree of statistical validity, a decision can be made to consider whether or not to mail any test list that has a dupe rate of under 15 percent. It's less costly to pay list rental costs than to mail at $300 per thousand. *There is a caveat:* The size and scope of the internal file does make a difference.

4. As part of the information stream, do a *yearly audit* of the tests conducted that year—the cost versus rewards. Evaluate the associative process of one test to another. Evaluate the discrepancies—the affirmations and rejections—as a forward opportunity. Evaluate the dollars spent on testing minor variations in copy and package.

Take a critical look at all your tests. Were they conducted with valid quantities? Were the split tests selected with equal quantities and comparable names on each side and mailed on the same day? Were the differences in response really significant? As a rule of thumb, any difference less than 15 percent is suspect. One of the dangers is that we test in great depth and sometimes do not take the time to analyze the results thoroughly. And test for breakthroughs, not trivia! Test quantitatively—assume nothing—and test again if results do not appear conclusive.

5. It is important to repeat that one of the great dangers is that we test in-depth but do not take the time to thoroughly analyze results. In instances where a company is entering the field for the first time, wrong conclusions can lead to wrong decisions. The primary objective of a test is to isolate the factors which work. Assuming that the direct mail plan was tied into the overall marketing objectives, you can't just look at the bottom line (the averages). Averages can be misleading.

Look at the components. Were there three to four lists with sufficient universe which were responsive? Did one or two copy and offer cells appear to be relatively successful? If so, these alternatives should be explored further even though the bottom-line total result appears to be unsatisfactory.

SYLLOGISM

Direct mail is a measurable medium, but neither our successes nor our failures teach us much if we don't learn to qualify as well as quantify our responses. Without careful attention to the meaning of our results leading to deductive reasoning, we have no basis for long-term planning; and short-term planning can be deceptive and financially exhausting. You can't predict if you don't prepare.

To quote John Adams: "Facts are stubborn things, and whatever may be our wishes, our inclination or the dictates of our passions, they cannot alter the state of the facts and the evidence."

Seasonality Study

A NEWS SERVICE OF **THE KLEID COMPANY INC.** 200 PARK AVENUE, NEW YORK, NY 10166 (212) 599-4140

office of the president

Volume III, No. 8

April 1985

Seasonality Study / Update #9

To perceive the future possibilities of the effect of seasonality on mailing programs, it helps to observe seasonal trends.

While our analysis demonstrates a strong general relationship between product category and timing, there are some variations. Seasonality (as is true of other elements in direct mail) does not proceed in discrete logical steps.

Clearly the implications of the Seasonality/Profitability relationship can vary according to the planning dynamics (or constraints) of the individual company. However, variations are present in reviewing the five-year figures and can be directional when mailings are being budgeted and the mail date decided upon.

Note the chart below:

	1984-1985		5 Year Average	
	Top Month	# 2 Month	Top Month	# 2 Month
Business & Finance	December	June	December	January
Cultural Reading	December	June	December	June
General Reading	December	June	December	June
Self Improvement	December	July	December	January
Home Interest	July	October	December	January
Parents & Children	July	January	July	January
Hobbies	December	July	July	December
Entertainment	December	July/Jan.	December	July/Jan.
Education, Tech.	June	December	December	June
Fund Raising	September	October	September	January

One of the reasons for the strength and persistency of December is because many mailers are dropping before and immediately after Christmas in preference to January.

For those of you receiving this study for the first time this analysis, while based on volume, is enhanced by a comparison to actual response developed internally. This response correlation covers a representative sampling of companies within the spectrum of product categories. On this basis there is a correlation between the volume criteria used in this study and response.

We do hope you find this study of interest.

Rose Harper

C.R. Harper / President

<u>SEASONALITY STUDY</u>
<u>CATEGORY: BUSINESS/FINANCE</u>

MONTHLY % OF TOTAL MAILINGS

	1980-81	1981-82	1982-83	1983-84	1984-85	5-Year Average
MAR	8.7	6.2	11.2	8.1	4.7	7.8
APR	7.0	8.7	4.6	5.7	7.5	6.7
MAY	3.5	8.4	6.0	6.3	4.8	5.8
JUNE	6.1	5.9	7.6	9.1	11.4	8.0
JULY	8.7	9.4	7.9	9.1	6.7	8.4
AUG	5.3	6.9	6.3	4.5	5.8	5.8
SEPT	10.4	8.5	9.3	7.4	6.5	8.4
OCT	5.6	8.0	7.1	10.6	9.5	8.2
NOV	4.3	5.8	4.2	4.7	6.7	5.1
DEC	11.9	14.2	15.6	14.7	18.3	14.9
JAN	19.7	11.0	13.1	13.8	8.6	13.2
FEB	8.8	7.0	7.1	6.0	9.5	7.7
TOTAL	100%	100%	100%	100%	100%	100%

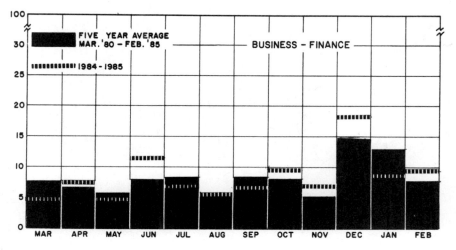

Comments:

December clearly the winner with an all time high in 1984 of 18.3% while
January slipped to its lowest level in five years. June is continuing on
its upward trend having grown by two-fold since 1981.

SEASONALITY STUDY
CATEGORY: CULTURAL READING

MONTHLY % OF TOTAL MAILINGS

--------------------------------- .------

	1980-81	1981-82	1982-83	1983-84	1984-85	5-Year Average
MAR	2.4	4.0	6.4	4.1	4.2	4.2
APR	2.4	2.1	1.6	6.8	1.5	2.9
MAY	1.9	1.6	.4	2.2	1.8	1.5
JUNE	12.0	14.5	15.6	14.6	13.6	14.1
JULY	15.1	8.6	6.6	7.2	9.0	9.3
AUG	10.9	3.4	2.9	4.4	4.2	5.2
SEPT	8.0	13.4	10.4	10.1	10.5	10.5
OCT	6.7	7.8	11.3	7.0	7.1	8.0
NOV	4.9	4.6	2.1	3.5	7.0	4.4
DEC	21.4	21.1	33.5	25.9	22.6	24.9
JAN	8.0	9.4	6.4	10.7	10.5	9.0
FEB	6.3	9.5	2.8	3.5	8.0	6.0
TOTAL	100%	100%	100%	100%	100%	100%

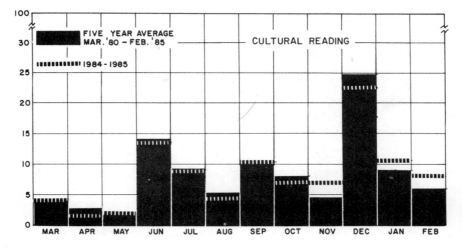

Comments:

December followed by June appear to be the best two months. However the difference between these months is substantial.

SEASONALITY STUDY
CATEGORY: GENERAL READING

MONTHLY % OF TOTAL MAILINGS

	1980-81	1981-82	1982-83	1983-84	1984-85	5-Year Average
MAR	9.8	3.5	11.4	10.1	4.8	7.9
APR	3.9	1.5	2.7	3.6	7.1	3.8
MAY	2.3	3.5	8.2	5.9	10.1	6.0
JUNE	12.5	3.1	18.2	11.3	16.0	12.2
JULY	19.3	26.0	8.6	13.3	12.3	15.9
AUG	4.5	2.4	3.5	2.8	2.3	3.1
SEPT	12.0	11.9	7.6	11.3	8.8	10.3
OCT	1.6	0.1	0.9	3.0	1.7	1.5
NOV	0.8	1.9	0.1	1.9	2.0	1.3
DEC	16.4	22.6	21.4	25.8	20.4	21.3
JAN	12.7	18.8	12.5	7.0	12.0	12.6
FEB	4.2	4.7	4.9	4.0	2.5	4.1
TOTAL	100%	100%	100%	100%	100%	100%

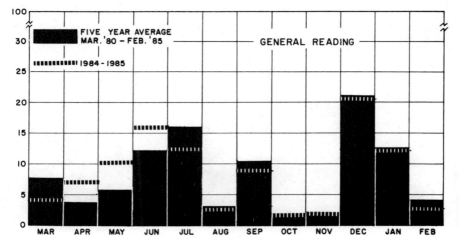

FIVE YEAR AVERAGE MAR. '80 – FEB. '85 — GENERAL READING

1984-1985

Comments:

December, although somewhat lower from preceding year, still is best.
June is again in second place after losing to July last year. Along with
Jan. and May, these five months account for 70% of the total volume in
this category.

SEASONALITY STUDY
CATEGORY: SELF-IMPROVEMENT

MONTHLY % OF TOTAL MAILINGS

	1980-81	1981-82	1982-83	1983-84	1984-85	5-Year Average
MAR	9.0	2.2	5.8	6.7	4.8	5.7
APR	7.8	2.4	3.1	5.7	8.2	5.4
MAY	2.1	1.5	2.2	5.1	1.8	2.5
JUNE	4.3	5.6	6.8	10.8	14.2	8.3
JULY	12.1	7.3	5.1	2.6	14.9	8.4
AUG	3.6	9.0	10.8	11.0	3.6	7.6
SEPT	6.1	15.9	14.2	11.6	11.2	11.8
OCT	4.0	1.3	7.3	7.0	6.3	5.2
NOV	2.3	1.6	2.9	1.1	1.4	2.0
DEC	14.7	30.8	16.3	14.9	19.5	19.2
JAN	23.3	13.1	14.3	14.0	10.1	15.0
FEB	10.7	9.3	11.2	9.5	4.0	8.9
TOTAL	100%	100%	100%	100%	100%	100%

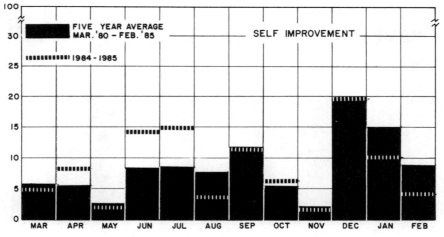

Comments:

Note the dramatic rise in July and June now #2 and #3 respectively behind
December (#1) which rose significantly from last year's level. Meanwhile,
Jan. and Feb. continue to lose ground.

SEASONALITY STUDY
CATEGORY: HOME INTEREST

MONTHLY % OF TOTAL MAILINGS

	1980-81	1981-82	1982-83	1983-84	1984-85	5-Year Average
MAR	6.2	2.6	2.0	4.8	7.9	4.7
APR	5.0	5.3	4.1	3.3	6.0	4.7
MAY	1.2	2.4	1.4	2.8	1.8	1.9
JUNE	0.7	8.9	13.2	10.0	11.3	8.9
JULY	6.7	12.4	9.9	15.2	20.0	12.8
AUG	7.7	8.9	9.2	9.3	6.3	8.3
SEPT	14.0	9.7	7.0	12.8	6.4	10.0
OCT	10.4	8.9	9.8	10.2	12.2	10.3
NOV	0.6	0.9	1.9	1.1	3.3	1.6
DEC	14.3	7.0	20.4	16.0	11.7	13.9
JAN	18.8	14.8	15.3	10.3	10.0	13.8
FEB	14.4	18.2	5.8	4.2	3.1	9.1
TOTAL	100%	100%	100%	100%	100%	100%

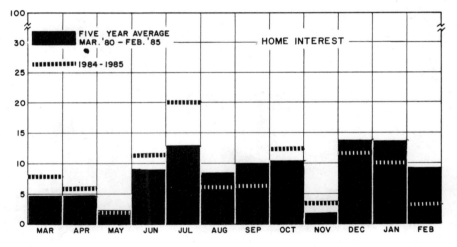

Comments:

Note the significant strength of July emerging as #1 and the relative
weakness of December dropping to #3 from the top spot 2 years in a row.
June, Oct. and Jan. are also popular.

SEASONALITY STUDY
CATEGORY: PARENTS AND CHILDREN

MONTHLY % OF TOTAL MAILINGS

	1980-81	1981-82	1982-83	1983-84	1984-85	5-Year Average
MAR	2.5	2.5	3.2	2.4	3.0	2.7
APR	1.0	1.4	0.9	1.0	.8	1.1
MAY	5.2	8.4	8.5	2.2	2.7	5.4
JUNE	3.1	3.3	3.3	5.7	8.6	4.8
JULY	19.7	23.2	18.6	27.1	20.8	21.9
AUG	15.2	12.3	11.3	10.5	12.1	12.3
SEPT	2.9	1.7	5.0	5.7	7.9	4.6
OCT	3.4	2.9	1.2	1.0	1.6	2.0
NOV	1.5	0.4	0.5	2.5	2.6	1.5
DEC	23.7	13.6	17.9	11.7	12.2	15.8
JAN	19.0	18.9	15.2	21.4	14.2	17.7
FEB	2.8	11.4	14.4	8.8	13.5	10.2
TOTAL	100%	100%	100%	100%	100%	100%

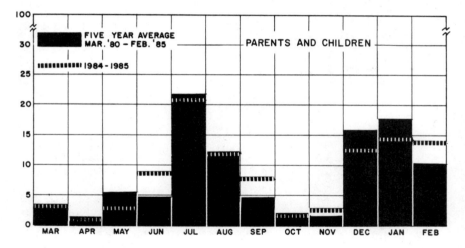

Comments:

Traditionally the four top months are July, Aug., Dec. and Jan. This year
Feb. looks good again. June and Sept. are in a positive trend.

SEASONALITY STUDY
CATEGORY: HOBBIES - RELATED SUBJECTS

MONTHLY % OF TOTAL MAILINGS

	1980-81	1981-82	1982-83	1983-84	1984-85	5-Year Average
MAR	6.8	3.8	2.3	3.9	8.5	5.1
APR	2.3	3.2	5.0	2.2	1.6	2.9
MAY	5.3	3.8	3.0	2.2	2.4	3.3
JUNE	2.8	6.5	4.2	5.7	12.3	6.3
JULY	22.8	22.9	17.3	20.2	16.1	19.9
AUG	8.9	7.2	8.3	8.9	10.5	8.8
SEPT	6.4	9.0	11.7	5.1	5.6	7.6
OCT	2.0	2.5	2.8	8.6	5.3	4.2
NOV	0.9	0.8	2.7	1.0	.5	1.0
DEC	14.8	17.4	20.6	23.9	20.1	19.4
JAN	21.3	15.5	15.2	12.0	8.8	14.6
FEB	5.7	7.4	6.9	6.3	8.3	6.9
TOTAL	100%	100%	100%	100%	100%	100%

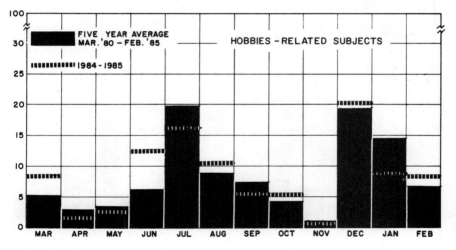

Comments:

The traditional seasonal trend seems undisturbed except for the new high reached by June. (Note that June was strong in several other categories.)

SEASONALITY STUDY
CATEGORY: ENTERTAINMENT

MONTHLY % OF TOTAL MAILINGS

	1980-81	1981-82	1982-83	1983-84	1984-85	5-Year Average
MAR	3.1	7.1	2.7	3.2	9.3	5.1
APR	0.9	5.1	3.2	4.1	3.1	3.3
MAY	1.7	2.3	3.1	3.9	5.0	3.1
JUNE	2.3	4.5	8.9	4.8	7.8	5.7
JULY	15.0	17.5	13.1	10.1	9.8	13.1
AUG	4.4	13.8	7.3	8.2	8.2	8.4
SEPT	15.3	12.0	11.0	9.9	8.3	11.3
OCT	6.6	8..	8.9	10.1	6.9	8.2
NOV	7.2	5.0	2.2	6.0	1.7	4.4
DEC	14.9	8.7	17.3	23.7	21.6	17.2
JAN	19.1	7.4	16.6	12.5	9.8	13.1
FEB	9.5	8.2	5.7	3.5	8.5	7.1
TOTAL	100%	100%	100%	100%	100%	100%

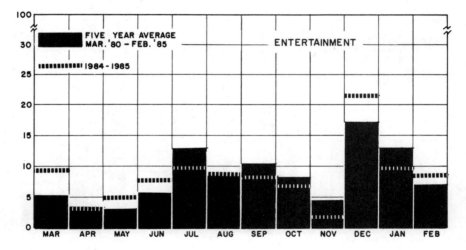

Comments:

After hitting a low in the 1981-82 period, December emerged as "numero uno" in the last 3 years. In 1984, it accounted for 22% of the total mailings exceeding the nearest competitors July and Jan. by almost 12 percentage points.

SEASONALITY STUDY
CATEGORY: EDUCATIONAL, TECHNICAL, PROFESSIONAL

MONTHLY % OF TOTAL MAILINGS

	1980-81	1981-82	1982-83	1983-84	1984-85	5-Year Average
MAR	2.6	4.4	8.2	6.6	8.5	6.1
APR	3.7	8.4	6.1	3.9	13.5	7.1
MAY	3.9	1.1	3.0	5.6	8.1	4.3
JUNE	3.8	33.2	9.5	3.5	15.9	13.2
JULY	12.1	9.9	1.7	9.4	5.6	7.7
AUG	10.2	3.6	8.7	11.4	4.5	7.7
SEPT	5.3	4.5	8.5	10.9	7.8	7.4
OCT	9.1	9.0	6.4	10.7	8.5	8.7
NOV	7.6	4.9	9.8	4.0	5.5	6.4
DEC	27.1	10.5	9.9	14.6	15.0	15.4
JAN	9.3	5.3	19.6	12.9	3.3	10.1
FEB	5.3	5.2	8.6	6.5	3.8	5.9
TOTAL	100%	100%	100%	100%	100%	100%

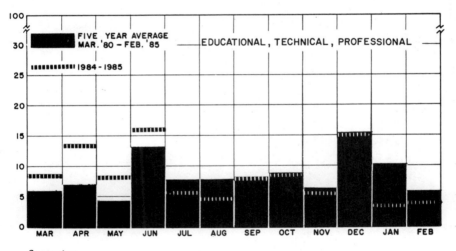

Comments:

June and December stand out in this category whether you look at 1984-85 or
the 5-year average. But April is swinging up having more than tripled last
year's percentage. It will be interesting to see if this strength
continues in 1985.

SEASONALITY STUDY
CATEGORY: FUND RAISING

MONTHLY % OF TOTAL MAILINGS

	1980-81	1981-82	1982-83	1983-84	1984-85	5-Year Average
MAR	6.4	6.3	10.9	5.9	6.3	7.2
APR	3.4	6.6	5.5	5.5	9.2	6.0
MAY	5.5	5.4	6.0	3.6	5.6	5.2
JUNE	1.3	1.7	4.2	6.9	9.1	4.6
JULY	0.8	7.1	5.9	1.6	2.7	3.7
AUG	8.4	11.3	6.8	9.4	10.0	9.2
SEPT	11.6	10.6	13.3	8.3	12.7	11.3
OCT	10.3	11.5	8.9	13.2	11.5	11.1
NOV	9.3	13.6	9.0	12.0	9.9	10.8
DEC	7.9	6.6	10.8	14.0	4.9	8.8
JAN	29.6	6.4	6.4	5.6	8.2	11.2
FEB	5.5	12.9	12.3	14.0	9.9	10.9
TOTAL	100%	100%	100%	100%	100%	100%

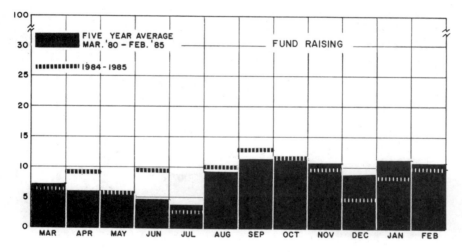

Comments:

Sept., Oct., August (top 3 months) account for 34.2% of the total. Nov.,
Feb., April, June represent 38.1%. It does seem that on a quantitative
basis there is no definite seasonality pattern.

CHAPTER 9

List Testing: Science or Art?

Some early literature treats list testing as a rule-of-thumb exercise. Those days are gone forever. Today we speak more and more about probabilities rather than certainties. The competition is heavy, the consumer more discriminating, and the risks large. To survive, let alone thrive, in today's direct mail marketing environment requires a high level of professionalism. New skills must be mastered, knowledge acquired, and systems developed. The fast-changing electronic technologies are creating opportunities to address the provocative issue of *testing* which affects performance and productivity.

Technology has moved list testing and analysis to more of a "science" and less of an "art." But there's still a long road ahead. Why? The principal reason is that list tests are not conducted under controlled laboratory conditions. There are too many variables: size of the test, whether the cross-section of the list was truly representative, seasonality, change in promotion packages, change in offer, change in the makeup of the list itself, repeatability of names, etc. Considering the influence of these factors, test results can't always be projected with a high degree of accuracy. That's a fact. *The answer:* Estimating response can be reduced to tolerable and manageable levels with a better understanding and application of probability and statistical theories.

Much has been written about list testing and evaluation, some of it rather confusing because probability and statistics must be applied and these are difficult subjects (for many) to understand.

Much contradictory material has been published. Are test mailing sizes really dependent upon the list universe? If so, why do we retest larger lists? To a great extent the mathematics used in direct mail has been adapted by people who know a great deal about statistics but usually less about direct mail. On the other hand, many direct mail practitioners tend to be intimidated by statistics and related subjects and accept inadequate or erroneous guidelines or misuse valid ones.

In direct mail, lists are where the customers and the sales are. Even when all the other elements are flawlessly executed, the failure to properly test and evaluate lists can be detrimental to the health of your next direct mail campaign. Therefore, it is essential to strive for better understanding of the available predictive techniques.

Let's take a closer look at the fundamental concepts of probability and statistics and the basic principles that apply to direct mail. There is no need to be intimidated. An elementary knowledge of only a few items is all that is required. No need to become a Ph.D. candidate—if parts of the material become somewhat difficult to follow, you can concentrate on the basics.

DEFINITIONS

Probability, in statistics, means the relative possibility that an event will occur, as expressed by the ratio of the number of actual occurrences to the total number of possible occurrences, in other words, the relative frequency with which an event occurs or is likely to occur.

A *statistic* is a numerical fact or datum. *Statistics* is the science that deals with the collection, classification, analysis, and interpretation of numerical facts or data. Statistics, by use of mathematical theories of probability, imposes order and regularity on aggregates of more or less disparate elements.

BASIC CONCEPTS OF PROBABILITY AND STATISTICS

Think of a number. Then double it. Add 10 to it. Divide by 2. Subtract the first number you thought of, and the answer will always be 5. Wouldn't it be easy if the law of probability were always so simple?

RANDOMNESS

There are two common types of phenomena observed in human experience. One is predictable and deterministic. The properties can be measured directly or indirectly and either remain fixed or vary according to a specific mechanism. Once that mechanism is well-understood, prediction of the future values of the properties can readily be made. For example, the area of a rectangular field can always be calculated by multiplying the length by the width.

The other type of phenomenon is characterized by series of events which appear to occur in a haphazard manner but which are definitively fixed as to their possible distinct forms. These seemingly haphazard, or random, occurrences introduce elements of uncertainty and, therefore, risk. Will the crops be good this year? Will a tornado hit my home? How do I place my bets so I can win before I lose my bankroll? Can I sell enough Handy Dandy pocket gadgets to the people on this mailing list to turn a profit?

One of these questions so intrigued mathematicians that they developed probability and statistics to reduce as much as possible the uncertainty inherent in random occurrences. The crucial concept here is the reduction of risk and not the elimination of it. Risk is eliminated only in deterministic events. To reduce the risk of mailing in a random universe, the theory of probability and statistics must be employed.

WHAT IS PROBABILITY?

Central to random phenomenon is the concept of probability. "Probability" is one of the most confusing and misunderstood terms. We can say when flipping a coin that the probability of tossing a head is one-half (assuming a fair coin). Can we predict the outcome of the next toss? Not at all! What about the roll of a nonloaded die? The probability of rolling a 1 is one-sixth. Can we predict the next roll? Still no. So, what is probability, and how do we use it?

If we were to start tossing our coin repeatedly and recording the outcomes, we would notice that, after a large number of tosses, the proportion of heads to total tosses was a number fairly close to one-half (or .5). Not exactly .5, but close to it. As we continue to experiment, the proportion of heads to total tosses tends, in an irregular fashion, to approach more and more closely the value .5. In the limit of the experiment, as the number of tosses becomes very large (infinity in theory), the value approaches .5 so closely as to be indistinguishable from it. This is the definition and meaning of "probability."

To illustrate this point, Chart 9.1 tabulates the results of simulating a coin toss 500,000 times. The ratio of heads does not appear to settle down

Chart 9.1   Coin Toss Simulation

No. of Tosses	Ratio of Heads	No. of Tosses	Ratio of Heads	No. of Tosses	Ratio of Heads
1	1.000000	100	.430000	10,000	.491500
2	1.000000	200	.465000	20,000	.499450
3	.666667	300	.450000	30,000	.496200
4	.500000	400	.477500	40,000	.496575
5	.400000	500	.462000	50,000	.496840
10	.300000	1000	.503000	100,000	.497200
20	.300000	2000	.496500	200,000	.497610
30	.333333	3000	.495333	300,000	.497367
40	.425000	4000	.496750	400,000	.497475
50	.400000	5000	.490800	500,000	.497465

until well after 1000 tosses and is still significantly different from the anticipated .5 after 500,000 tosses. Incidentally, can we tell from the results whether we are using a fair coin? The 95 percent confidence limits for 500,000 tosses turn out to be ± .001386. We are then 95 percent confident that the true probability of tossing a head lies in the interval .497465 ± .001386, or between .496079 and .498885. The conclusion is that our simulated coin, just a real coin, is slightly biased, in this case toward tails.

The probability of tossing a head with a fair coin, .5, is defined only in a limiting situation, and we must not expect to be able to accurately predict a few small events. Fortunately, the predictive attributes of probability begin to manifest themselves long before very large numbers of repetitions have occurred. *To illustrate:* We cannot predict the outcome of a single event (will the fifth name on the list respond?), but we can get a good feel for the outcome of a number of events (how many of the names will respond?). The larger the number of events, in our case, responses, the more confident we become in our predictions and the less risk we take.

WHAT ARE RANDOM VARIABLES AND DISTRIBUTIONS?

Random phenomena are analyzed by the study of the *behavior* of random variables. That can be quite a frightening term, but random variables are really quite benign. The variable simply assigns the probability of each possible outcome of a situation. It is called a "variable" because it defines more than one single outcome. It is "random" because it describes nondeterministic phenomena. Let's look at an example. If we were to flip our fair coin three times, there would be four possible outcomes: zero heads, one head, two heads, or three heads (assuming we are not interested in the order of the heads). The random variable used to describe this phenomenon can be called H, which may have a value of 0, 1, 2, or 3. The probability of H's assuming the value of 0, 1, 2, or 3 can then be assigned:

$$p\ (H = 0) = .125$$

The probability that H assumes value 0 (no heads in the tosses) is .125. The experiment results in 0 heads 125 times out of 1000, in the limit. Similarly:

$$p\ (H = 1) = .375$$

$$p\ (H = 2) = .375$$

$$p\ (H = 3) = .125$$

Note that the sum of all probabilities is 1. One or another of the outcomes must occur.

The probabilities associated with each outcome can be described by equations or tables which are called "distributions." Thus a random variable must have a specific range of values (outcomes) and a definable probability associated with each. In direct mail, a common random variable is the number of responses to an offer or the response rate. Random variables may behave according to many distributions, but in direct mail two are of importance.

THE BINOMIAL AND NORMAL DISTRIBUTIONS

Binomial. In statistics implies two possible outcomes which could be labeled "success" or "failure"

Binomial distribution. In statistics, a distribution giving the probability of obtaining a specified number of successes in a finite set of independent trials in which the probability of success remains the same from trial to trial

The number of heads in a series of tosses or the number of direct mail responses is described by the binomial distribution. Each individual on a list can be thought of as having a probability p of accepting the offer and of $1 - p$ of rejecting it. The value of p is not .5 but closer to .02 (2 of every 100 in the limit). The binomial distribution applies to events with two possible results: H or T, accept or reject. The *parameters*, or important distinguishing values of this distribution, are the number of events (names or tosses) called n and the probability p of a single outcome. If we mailed 10,000 names, the binomial distribution would tell us the probability of 0 responses, 1 response, etc., all the way to 10,000 responses. By adding up these probabilities, we can know, for instance, the probability of the responses numbering 10, 11, or 12 or between 50 and 100, or whatever interval we may be interested in. This is exactly what we need.

Unfortunately, the binomial distribution has a real flaw. The calculations rapidly become too complex because they involve factorials of n. If you don't know what that is, just accept the fact that calculating the factorial of 5000 is no fun.

As it turns out, the binomial can be closely approximated by a well-known and analyzed distribution called the "normal." The normal is easy to use and is employed in list testing. The approximation breaks down for values of $n \times p$ of less than 5. However, in direct mail this implies n less than 500 names and therefore introduces no problem since test quantities are substantially greater.

Normal distributions are defined by two parameters: the mean m and the standard deviation s. Mathematicians prefer to use the symbols μ (mu) and σ (sigma).

Look at the plot of a normal distribution shown in Chart 9.2. The curve gives the probability of the random variable assuming a value x. The curve is symmetrical about $x = m$ (the most probable value of x) and falls off rapidly with increasing distance from m. The rapidity of this decrease is controlled by the standard deviation s. The larger the standard deviation, the more spread out the distribution (Chart 9.3).

We are less interested in calculating the probability of a single value of x (who cares if exactly 503 people respond) than in calculating the probability, say, that the number responding will be between 450 and 550. If that

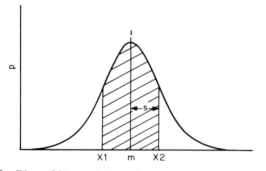

Chart 9.2   Plot of Normal Distribution

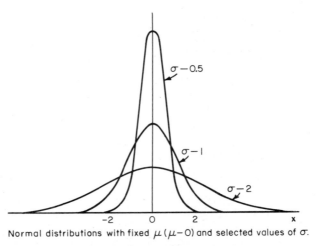

Normal distributions with fixed μ (μ-0) and selected values of σ.

**Chart 9.3   The Larger the Standard Deviation, the
More Spread Out the Distribution**

probability were .95, we could then say that 95 percent of the time the
number of responses would be between 450 and 550.

The probability of the random variable x lying between $x1$ and $x2$ is
defined by the area under the curve between $x1$ and $x2$ (Chart 9.2). The
calculations of these areas are quite intricate, but fortunately they have
been published in the form of tables.

To reduce the volume of printed material, only the standard normal
tables are utilized. The *standard normal* is a normal with $m = 0$ and $s = 1$.
Other normals can be scaled to the standard normal so that the standard
tables may be used. Individuals involved in list testing and evaluating
should learn how to use these tables by consulting appropriate reference
material.

It is interesting to note that most of the area under the curve lies within
a few standard deviations from the mean. The total area under the curve
is defined as 1 (Chart 9.4). Thus the probability of x's lying within 1
standard deviation on either side of the mean is .6827. This is always true
regardless of the size of the standard deviation.

The mean of the normal distribution applicable in direct mail is equal to
np, that is, the number of names mailed times the probability of response
(or success rate). The standard deviation is equal to $\sqrt{np(1 - p)}$. (The
symbol $\sqrt{}$ is the square root sign.) For example, if $n = 5000$
names and response is .02, then m (mean) $= 5000 \times .02 = 100$, and $s =
\sqrt{5000 \times .02 \times .98} = 9.899$.

The normal distribution tells us that 68.27 percent of the time the

Chart 9.4   Deviations from the Mean

No. of Standard Deviations from Mean	Area
.5	.3829
1.0	.6827
1.5	.8664
2.0	.9545
3.0	.9973

response would lie between m plus or minus s, which is 100 ± 9.899 or between 90 and 110. The factor $(1 - p)$ is so close to 1 that it may be left out of the equation without affecting the results very much. Thus $s = \sqrt{np}$ may be used.

There are many other distribution extensions in nature. Some of them are not symmetrical like the normal. They are "skewed," which means that these distributions are not evenly distributed about the mean. They give greater weight to one side or the other.

Many of us have wondered about the significance of skewed distributions in direct mail. Rollouts often appear to lie preponderantly on the low side of test results. Could it be that the normal distribution may not be quite as applicable as previously thought?

ESTIMATION AND CONFIDENCE INTERVALS

A probability distribution may contain unknown parameters, such as the mean, which one would like to estimate. By "sampling the distribution," that is, extracting values from it, the true value of a single parameter can be bracketed by an interval usually called the "confidence interval." Elements of confidence and precision are brought into balance. We may, for instance, say that the 95 percent confidence interval for estimating the mean is ± 10. If the best estimate of the mean were 90, we would be 95 percent confident that the true value of the mean was between 80 and 100. But what does that really mean?

Let's look at a normal distribution with mean m of 100 and a standard deviation s of 10. We know from the tables that 68.27 percent of the area of the distribution lies within 1 standard deviation of the mean. Thus 68.27 percent of a large number of samples would have values between $m - s$ and $m + s$ (between 90 and 110). In each of these cases the true value of the mean 100 would be within s (i.e., 10) of the sample value. We would then say that we are 68.27 percent confident that the true mean lies within s of the sample value.

Since 95.45 percent of the curve lies within 2 standard deviations of the mean, we can say that we are 95.45 percent confident that the true mean lies within 2 standard deviations of the sample value (between 80 and 120). Here we are more confident (95.45 to 68.27 percent) that our hypothesis is correct, but the precision of our estimate has been cut in half (from 1 standard deviation to 2). Let's look at a direct mail example.

We know that the standard deviation in terms of responses is given by $s = \sqrt{np(1 - p)}$. Responses are less meaningful though than response rate. To get the standard deviation in terms of response rate Sr, we divide by total number of offers n.

$$Sr = \frac{s}{n} = \sqrt{\frac{np(1 - p)}{n}} = \sqrt{p\frac{(1 - p)}{n}}$$

We can express the confidence interval (also called "limits") in terms of the number of standard deviations, let's call it Z_c, associated with a confidence level. As we previously saw, 1 standard deviation represents 68.27 percent confidence, and 2 represent 95.45 percent confidence. The equation defining the confidence limits then becomes:

$$L = \pm Z_c \sqrt{p\frac{(1 - p)}{n}}$$

This is the derivation of the formula commonly found in the literature and used to compile the tables of sample size and limit of error. It was presented here only for interest and to dispel its mystery. If the math was confusing, it doesn't matter. In practice, the confidence levels of interest are not 95.45 or 68.27 percent but 80 percent, 90 percent, 95 percent, and 99 percent. These correspond to values of Z_c of 1.282, 1.645, 1.960, and 2.576. Incidentally, the terms "confidence interval," "confidence limits," and "limits of error" are all synonymous.

Consider the following example. If the return rate is 2 percent and 5000 names are mailed, then the 95 percent confidence limits would be:

$$L = \pm 1.960 \times \text{square root of } (.02 \times \frac{1 - .02}{5000})$$
$$= \pm 1.960 \times \text{square root of } (.00000392)$$
$$= \pm 1.960 \times (.001979899)$$
$$= \pm .00388$$

In this case, 95 percent of the time the actual return from a mailing of 5000 names would lie between .02 + .00388 and .02 − .00388, or between 2.388 and 1.612 percent.

In practice, we do not know the true rate of return but want to estimate it so that we can evaluate the profit characteristics of lists. The return rate from a test gives us the best estimate of the true return rate within the limits and confidence levels just discussed. Users must balance the level of risk (confidence level) and the degree of precision (limits) to calculate a sample size n which will satisfy their needs. We can gain some insight into this problem by examining Chart 9.5, which is a table of confidence (or error) limits.

The first three entries show that the error limits expand with the confidence level, all other things being equal. We can be more confident if we decrease the precision of our expectations. The next three entries illustrate that sample size must be increased considerably to reduce the limits (i.e., increase the precision). To get twice the precision, we must quadruple the sample size. The last three entries show that even though the error limits are larger for higher return rates, they are actually smaller as a percentage of the return rate. A 1 percent return rate has ±27.6 percent limits compared to ±12 percent limits for a 5 percent rate. This suggests using larger test samples for high-ticket items which usually have lower return rates.

ARE THERE DIFFERENT KINDS OF CONFIDENCE INTERVALS?

The confidence intervals are calculated differently for different distributions. Attempts have been made to modify the normal distribution so that it might more closely apply to direct mail, and these have led to variations in the equations and tables of confidence intervals.

Chart 9.5   Table of Confidence or Error Limits

	True Return Rate	Confidence Level	Sample Size	Limits
1.	.02	90 percent	5,000	.00326
2.	.02	95 percent	5,000	.00388
3.	.02	99 percent	5,000	.00510
4.	.02	95 percent	5,000	.00388
5.	.02	95 percent	20,000	.00194
6.	.02	95 percent	80,000	.00097
7.	.01	95 percent	5,000	.00276
8.	.02	95 percent	5,000	.00388
9.	.05	95 percent	5,000	.00604

Often the differences involved are insignificant and not worth bother-ing about. The theoretical foundations for these revised limits are usually not presented, which makes evaluating their soundness difficult or im-possible. A good general rule is to be wary unless respected, favorable opinions can be found.

The search for practical and theoretically sound innovations should be encouraged. Until such times as they are found, it seems prudent to stay with standard and consistent equations and tables. The difference be-tween the many versions is not dramatic, and adjustments must be made in any case. So it probably does not matter which you use as long as you use the same ones consistently.

USING CONFIDENCE INTERVAL TABLES AND FORMULAS

Let's review how to use the formulas and tables for the calculations of sample size and confidence limits. There are two kinds of calculations to consider. We may want to find the sample size n which will give us a preselected value of L. Or we may want to know the limit associated with a particular sample size.

Formula

$$L = \pm Z_c \sqrt{\frac{p(1 - p)}{n}} \tag{9.1}$$

$$n = \left(\frac{Z_c}{L}\right)^2 p(1 - p) \tag{9.2}$$

where L = confidence interval or error limits
$\quad n$ = sample size
$\quad p$ = response rate (not percentage)
$\quad Z_c$ = the confidence level, described in terms of the number of standard deviations (1.645 for 90 percent confidence, 1.960 for 95 percent, and 2.576 for 99 percent)

If $p = .02$ and $n = 5000$, then the value of L at 95 percent confidence using Equation 9.1 is

$$L = 1.96 \sqrt{\frac{.02 \times .98}{5000}} = .00388$$

1. Multiply .02 by $1 - .02$ (.0196).
2. Divide the result by 5000 (.00000392).

3. Take the square root of the result (.001979899).
4. Multiply by 1.96 (.00388).

Note: Use a calculator for computing the square root.

The value of n which will give an $L = .004$ at 95% confidence using Equation 9.2 is

$$n = \left(\frac{1.96}{.004}\right)^2 \times .02 \times .98 = 4706$$

1. Divide 1.96 by .004 (490).
2. Multiply the result by itself (240,100).
3. Multiply the result by .02 (4802).
4. Multiply the result by $1 - .02$ (4706).

Tables

The charts in Appendix 9A are from the *Direct Mail and Mail Order Handbook.* Here the response rates are in percentages (0.02 equals 2 percent) rather than ratios. Each table is identified by its confidence level or factor of confidence printed at the top. The columns represent the confidence limits, and the rows the response rates. The columns are identified by the top row and the rows by the left-hand column.

1. The number of names which must be mailed to ensure limits of $\pm.4$ percent at 95 percent confidence if the expected return rate is 2 percent can be found at the intersection of the 0.4 column and 2.0 row of the 95 percent confidence table. This intersection contains the number 4705. The result is the same as with the formula.
2. Finding the confidence limits is not quite as straightforward. To find the 95 percent confidence limits of a mailing of 5000 names with a return of 2 percent, the following procedure is employed. First the row labeled 2 percent is located on the 95 percent table. Then each successive intersection on that row is examined until the value closest to the mailing quantity is identified. In this case it is 4705. The column is then followed upward to read its heading, 0.40 percent in our case. If the sample size lies between two columns, interpolation between them may be performed.

MANAGING THE ELEMENTS THAT GO INTO OBJECTIVE FORECASTING

Expectations are often based on unrealistic appraisals or erroneous testing and analysis. It is not surprising in these cases that continuations fail to achieve the expected performance. The remedy appears simple. Develop better skills and apply them correctly. Yet it seems that no matter how accurately "classical" testing is performed, the results from list test to continuation rarely fall within the acceptable limits. Why? The answer seems obvious. Direct mail is too complex to be accurately described by standard models. From a practical standpoint then, one must try to understand and identify the "influencers" so that methods of dealing with them may be developed.

Some effects may be quantified and incorporated into equations as correction factors. Seasonality is a good example. Others defy positive identification and must be viewed as simply adding to the degree of uncertainty and risk. This suggests a widening of the confidence limits or a reduction of the confidence level. If we find that, after applying all known correction factors, the variations in result are 1.5 times, say, the theoretical 95 percent confidence limit, then this expanded limit is the one that should be used.

Let's examine some of the most probable causes of deviations from anticipated results.

RANDOM SAMPLE SELECTION

The sample chosen must be a random representative sample of the list. The Nth-name sample is the most common type of selection and is one of the easiest and most adequate methods of fulfilling these requirements. Nth-name random samples may be properly selected as follows: First the value of N is calculated by dividing the sample size into the universe of that portion of the list to be tested. Thus, for a sample of 5000 names from a list of 965,000 names, N is 965,000/5000, or 193. If the sample is composed of every 193rd name, it will be representative of the entire list, no matter how that list is arranged.

The starting place for the random search is of importance because of the many requests for test samples of standard, size, such as 5000 or 10,000. To prevent the same collection of names appearing in these samples, the starting point should be advanced from the first to the second, to the third, etc. names for each successive selection. The delivery of perfect samples may not be guaranteed by list owners, but at least insist that lists under your control, such as house lists, be properly processed.

Other methods, such as using the last digits of the Zip code, are sometimes employed. Populations are not randomly distributed across Zip codes, however, and one should be aware that Zip-code-selected random samples will tend to be biased. Also, preselected test samples which are provided to a number of users obviously create a prejudice.

Try to estimate the degree of integrity of your test sample. An inadequate one should lead you to expand the confidence limits. By how much? Ten percent, 20 percent, more? This is a subjective decision which must be made separately for each case in the light of experience.

INCORRECTLY APPLIED THEORY

As we have already seen, the normal distribution used in calculations is based on the binomial distribution, which describes single events that either occur or do not occur. The formulas apply only when this dichotomy is achieved. If order size is an important factor, or conversion and renewal of subscriptions, the equations and tables do not apply. They may be indicative of the results to be expected, but, unless the dichotomy can somehow be restored, they will be misleading. How is dichotomy restored? We may say that an order below a certain level is to be counted as just as much of a failure as no order at all. For example, an order below $10 is a failure, and above $10, a success. Or after the conversion series, we may label a nonconverted trial as a failure and a converted one a success.

Tables and formulas must be utilized in a consistent manner. Two different tables may yield slightly different confidence limits and sample sizes. Once one of them has been selected, it must be consistently used. Don't compare tests analyzed with different tables. The results will lose significance. This does not mean, however, that if you locate a table which seems to work better for you, you shouldn't use it. By all means explore the field, but do so in a sound manner. "Running parallel" is always a safe method of testing new concepts and tools.

The tables and formulas are predicated on paradigms that only approximate the real world. Some of these may be more suited than others in describing behavior of specific lists and products, but all suffer from varying degrees of inadequacy. The problem is fundamental. The direct mail environment is too complex to be accurately modeled by a single normal or related distribution. A list population is not really composed of black balls and red balls, of heads and tails, of individuals with a fixed probability of accepting the offer.

At any single point in time, it can be better represented by a combination of large numbers of subpopulations each with its own distributions and parameters. The art of demographics attempts to isolate and deal with some of these major subgroups. Furthermore, the characteristics of individuals which result in a disposition to respond to an offer do not remain fixed but are in a constant state of flux affected by randomly varying factors. How can we hope that a theory developed for stable and highly constrained systems could adequately describe this fluid situation? Attempts to incorporate these effects have been made in the past, but none with proven satisfactory results. Until real theoretical progress is made, what can be done to cope with this now?

We may not know the identity of the complex joint distribution, but we can guess that it must have a standard deviation considerably larger than the classical normal. Since the confidence limits are a function of the standard deviation, the thing to do is to utilize larger limits. How much larger depends on a number of factors linked to the volatility of the list and also of the product. Experience and analysis of historical data is the best guide here. Known quantifiable adjustments, such as seasonality, should be applied to historical data before analyzing it further to extract the expansion of limits.

Incidentally, the true complex distribution may very well turn out to be skewed rather than symmetrical. If this is so, the tendency of rollouts to be consistently below test estimates might, at least partially, be fundamental in nature.

AFTER ALL IS SAID AND DONE

How big should a sample be? The proper sample size is determined by two factors: sampling tolerance (or deviation) and the degree of risk that the user is willing to accept. As long as we have perfect random samples, we can keep sampling tolerance small by taking large samples. This part of the equation is scientific.

The risk factor is much harder to deal with because this involves subjective judgments. Some companies can't tolerate much risk. The acceptable risk depends on what you are testing. On a package test, you can stand rather large sampling tolerances, whereas price tests generally require high accuracy. (You may be living with that price decision for a long time.) List testing is something else with its own special rules and techniques.

Actually, the usual list test presents problems that statisticians and tables can't really cope with. List testing is not conducted under laboratory conditions nor are tests drawn on a true random basis. The closest is systematic sampling known as the "Nth sample," as previously discussed.

One way that has been suggested for getting a better feeling for the "validity" of a test is to request on a 5000 test two Nth-name samplings of 2500 each; on a 10,000 test, five Nth-name samples of 2000 each. Obviously, each cell must be keyed separately. If there are substantial variations within these subsets, you might consider a retest. Bear in mind that this is not intended as a statistical "value-added" technique because of error limits and small sample size. For example, the 95 percent limits for 2000 names and return rate of 2 percent are ± 0.6 percent; thus the individual subsets could have a response rate range of 1.4 to 2.6 percent without indications that anything was out of the ordinary. Therefore, the "feeling of validity" may be just an illusion. However, this approach, let us say, might just be cautionary in deciding on the continuation quantity.

Actually, a universal practice, depending on response, is to confirm the test with a larger sample. If the results hold up, it is relatively comfortable to proceed to the balance of the list or take another big bite based on response. For example, if a 1 percent response is acceptable and a list pulls 3 percent, you can go from a 10,000 test to 100,000 or more since you can afford a drop-off of 50 percent and still be above the acceptable response.

Sequential sampling is the most reliable schematic because you can schedule quantities on each successive usage in an orderly fashion, supported by monitored results. Thus, you are able to minimize and control the risks. The sequential sampling plan is vital on any program where persistency must be measured. Initial results can be misleading.

The "testing" question of "how many" will always be with us because it can't be answered in a universal positive way. There are no finite numbers of elements which are universally applicable to every product being sold by mail.

In general, then, for the list test, a 5000 quantity is usually adequate, and more than 10,000 doesn't seem to be worthwhile. Obviously, this is not true in all instances. A great deal depends on financial considerations, goals and objectives of the company involved, and the merge/purge rate or other exclusion devices. For example, if these exclusions run to about 20 percent or more, a 5000 sample would not be adequate. Relative to this, list tests should not be input at the tail end of the merge/purge but at the beginning of the file after the house lists. Otherwise, you will find that in some instances on a 5000 test you will mail 3000 names.

There is also another testing aspect involving lists which needs to be considered. If you're testing other elements (promotion packages, offer, price), there are two methods which can be used. The first involves extracting a random sample, say, 50,000, from the tape of names after all the lists have been merged and duplicate names eliminated. The same random quantity would be extracted for each of the tests plus the control* —and *mailed on the same day*. This is a valid theory if the lists you are mailing are representative of your market universe. If feasible, list identification should be kept as another evaluation measurement.

---

*"Control," in direct mail terms, represents the promotional package, offer, price, etc. against which the new approaches will be measured.

In situations, however, where one of the objectives is to develop targeted promotions to target markets (where there is a sufficient universe), the best approach is to extract samples for the test and the control from several lists which represent prime markets for your product or service.

Remember always that results can be interpreted better with a relatively small test whose biases are known than a larger test where you don't know how the sample was selected. And in package, offer, and price tests, beware of the "outliers" that can influence the *overall* average and can lead into completely wrong interpretations of results.

In science, it has been said that no experiment is a failure. This statement is possibly true since the scientists search for reasons why an experiment failed: contaminated cultures, imperfect sterilization, wrong-factor multiples, inadequate counts, and erroneous assumptions, and many other factors. The scientist's experiment is the mailer's test. And the primary thought is to think of it, and treat it just that way.

LIST PRETESTING: STILL TO COME

The concept of "pretesting" lists has been around for quite some time and is still in the developmental stage for a variety of reasons. The objective of pretesting is to find a method to determine whether a list will be responsive without mailing an entire test quantity of, say, 5000 or 10,000.

One approach is pretesting by telephone. Some experts in telephone marketing feel that there is a direct correlation between the response from a phone call versus a mailing. While the personal contact in a phone solicitation leads to a higher response, how much higher is open to question. Estimates range from 3 to 10 times greater. How does this relate to pretesting? With such a high rate of response, it would appear possible to achieve a pretty reliable reading from a smaller sample than required for a mailing. If statistical parameters can be established between phone and mail response, it could be possible to project results from the telephone sample. If positive, the balance of the names on the test list would be mailed. *Problem:* Most list owners do not approve telephone solicitation to their names (perhaps the small sample would be approved) and the extra time involved.

Another approach involves the formula used by TV networks to forecast election results based on "key precincts." If you can analyze your mailings to determine your own statistically valid key precincts, it would be possible to mail only small portions of a list to determine how the overall file will respond. This concept could also apply to tests of price, offer, copy, etc., as well as to lists.

Another (and perhaps) practical method involves a correlation based on the duplication rate between an outside list versus an active internal file (Chart 8.6). The premise is that a list which matches heavily against the house file implies a strong affinity relationship which could translate to good response. Conversely, if the match rate is low, the implication might be that the list does not represent the prospect. The end effect would be to mail only those lists which match at a predetermined rate or higher. This predetermined rate can be established only when response has been thoroughly analyzed and quantified on this basis. To pursue this concept requires a merge/purge system where duplicates can be apportioned on an equal and list-by-list basis.

APPENDIX 9A

Using Statistical Probability as a Tool

Charts 9A.1 through 9A.8 are from the *Direct Mail and Mail Order Handbook*. The response rates are given in percentages (0.02 equals 2 percent).

Chart 9A.1 Sample Size for Various Percentages of Expected Returns (P) and Limit of Error (E) if Factor of Confidence Is 95 Percent

P	0.01	0.02	0.03	0.04	0.05	0.06	0.07	0.08	0.09	0.10	0.12	0.14
0.1	383,716	95,929	42,635	23,982	15,349	10,659	7,831	5,995	4,737	13,837	2,665	1,957
0.2	766,664	191,666	85,185	47,916	30,667	21,296	15,646	11,979	9,465	7,667	5,324	3,911
0.3	1,148,843	287,211	127,649	71,803	45,954	31,912	23,445	17,951	14,183	11,488	7,978	5,861
0.4	1,530,254	382,564	170,028	95,641	61,210	42,507	31,229	23,910	18,892	15,303	10,627	7,807
0.5	1,910,898	477,724	212,321	119,431	76,436	53,080	38,998	29,858	23,591	19,109	13,270	9,749
0.6	2,290,772	572,693	254,530	143,173	91,631	63,632	46,750	35,793	28,281	22,908	15,908	11,687
0.7	2,669,879	667,470	296,653	166,867	106,795	74,163	54,487	41,717	32,961	26,699	18,541	13,622
0.8	3,048,218	762,054	338,690	190,514	121,929	84,673	62,208	47,628	37,632	30,482	21,168	15,552
0.9	3,425,788	856,447	380,643	214,112	137,032	95,160	69,913	53,528	42,294	34,258	23,790	17,478
1.0	3,802,590	950,648	422,510	237,662	152,104	105,628	77,604	59,415	46,945	38,026	26,407	19,401
1.1	4,178,624	1,044,656	464,290	261,164	167,145	116,072	85,277	65,291	51,587	41,786	29,018	21,319
1.2	4,553,890	1,138,472	505,987	284,618	182,156	126,496	92,936	71,155	56,220	45,539	31,624	23,234
1.3	4,928,387	1,232,097	547,598	308,024	197,135	136,899	100,579	77,006	60,844	49,284	34,225	25,145
1.4	5,302,116	1,325,529	589,123	331,382	212,085	147,280	108,206	82,845	65,458	53,021	36,820	27,051
1.5	5,675,078	1,418,769	630,564	354,692	227,003	157,640	115,818	88,673	70,062	56,751	39,410	28,954
1.6	6,047,270	1,511,818	671,919	377,954	241,891	167,980	123,413	94,489	74,657	60,473	41,995	30,853
1.7	6,418,695	1,604,674	713,187	401,168	256,748	178,297	130,993	100,292	79,243	64,187	44,574	32,748
1.8	6,789,352	1,697,338	754,372	424,334	271,574	188,592	138,557	106,083	83,819	67,894	47,148	34,639
1.9	7,159,240	1,789,810	795,471	447,452	286,370	198,868	146,106	111,863	88,386	71,592	49,717	36,526
2.0	7,528,360	1,882,090	836,483	470,523	301,134	209,121	153,640	117,631	92,942	75,284	52,280	38,410

E

2.1	7,896,712	1,974,178	877,412	493,544	315,868	219,352	161,157	123,386	97,490	78,967	54,838	40,289
2.2	8,264,296	2,066,074	918,255	516,518	330,572	229,564	168,659	129,129	102,028	82,643	57,391	42,165
2.3	8,631,111	2,157,778	959,010	539,444	345,244	239,753	176,144	134,861	106,556	86,311	59,938	44,036
2.4	8,997,158	2,249,290	999,683	562,322	359,886	249,920	183,614	140,581	111,076	89,972	62,480	45,903
2.5	9,362,438	2,340,609	1,040,271	585,152	374,498	260,068	191,069	146,288	115,585	93,624	65,017	47,767
2.6	9,726,948	2,431,737	1,080,770	607,934	389,078	270,192	198,508	151,983	120,085	97,269	67,547	49,627
2.7		2,522,673	1,121,187	630,668	403,628	280,296	205,932	157,667	124,576	100,907	70,074	51,483
2.8		2,613,416	1,161,518	653,354	418,147	290,380	213,340	163,339	129,058	104,537	72,595	53,335
2.9		2,703,968	1,201,761	675,992	432,635	300,440	220,732	168,998	133,528	108,159	75,110	55,183
3.0		2,794,328	1,241,922	698,582	447,092	310,480	228,107	174,645	137,990	111,773	77,620	57,026
3.1		2,884,495	1,281,998	721,124	461,519	320,499	235,468	180,281	142,443	115,380	80,125	58,867
3.2		2,974,470	1,321,984	743,618	475,915	330,496	242,813	185,904	146,886	118,979	82,623	60,702
3.3		3,064,264	1,361,889	766,063	490,281	340,371	250,141	191,516	151,320	122,570	85,118	62,535
3.4		3,153,845	1,401,709	788,461	504,615	350,427	257,456	197,115	155,745	126,154	87,607	64,364
3.5		3,243,244	1,441,439	810,811	518,919	360,360	264,754	202,703	160,160	129,730	90,089	66,188
3.6		3,332,452	1,481,088	833,113	533,192	370,271	272,036	208,278	164,565	133,298	92,568	68,009
3.7		3,421,467	1,520,652	855,367	547,435	380,163	279,303	213,842	168,961	136,859	95,041	69,825
3.8		3,510,290	1,560,125	877,572	561,646	390,031	286,553	219,393	173,346	140,412	97,507	71,638
3.9		3,598,92	1,599,519	899,730	575,827	399,878	293,788	224,932	177,723	143,957	99,969	73,446
4.0		3,687,860	1,638,826	921,840	589,978	409,706	301,007	230,460	182,091	147,494	102,426	75,252

Chart 9A.2 Sample Size for Various Percentages of Expected Returns (P) and Limit of Error (E) if Factor of Confidence Is 95 Percent

P	E 0.16	0.18	0.20	0.25	0.30	0.35	0.40	0.45	0.50	0.55	0.60	0.70
0.1	1,499	1,184	959	614	426	313	240	189	153	127	106	78
0.2	2,994	2,366	1,917	1,226	852	626	479	378	307	253	213	156
0.3	4,487	3,546	2,872	1,838	1,276	938	718	567	459	379	319	234
0.4	5,977	4,723	3,826	2,448	1,700	1,249	956	756	612	506	425	312
0.5	7,464	5,897	4,777	3,057	2,123	1,560	1,194	943	764	631	530	390
0.6	8,948	7,070	5,727	3,665	2,545	1,870	1,432	1,131	916	757	636	467
0.7	10,429	8,240	6,675	4,272	2,966	2,179	1,669	1,318	1,068	882	741	545
0.8	11,907	9,408	7,621	4,877	3,387	2,488	1,905	1,505	1,219	1,007	847	622
0.9	13,382	10,573	8,564	5,481	3,806	2,796	2,141	1,692	1,370	1,132	951	699
1.0	14,854	11,736	9,506	6,084	4,225	3,104	2,376	1,877	1,521	1,257	1,056	776
1.1	16,322	12,897	10,446	6,686	4,643	3,411	2,611	2,063	1,671	1,381	1,160	853
1.2	17,788	14,055	11,385	7,286	5,060	3,717	2,846	2,249	1,821	1,505	1,265	929
1.3	19,251	15,211	12,321	7,885	5,476	4,023	3,080	2,434	1,971	1,629	1,369	1,006
1.4	20,711	16,364	13,255	8,483	5,891	4,328	3,314	2,618	2,121	1,753	1,473	1,082
1.5	22,168	17,515	14,188	9,080	6,305	4,632	3,547	2,802	2,270	1,876	1,576	1,158
1.6	23,622	18,664	15,118	9,675	6,719	4,936	3,780	2,986	2,419	1,999	1,680	1,234

1.7	1,310	1,783	2,122	2,567	3,170	4,012	5,240	7,132	10,270	16,047	19,811	25,073
1.8	1,385	1,886	2,244	2,716	3,352	4,243	5,542	7,543	10,863	16,973	20,955	26,521
1.9	1,461	1,988	2,366	2,868	3,535	4,474	5,844	7,955	11,455	17,898	22,096	27,966
2.0	1,536	2,091	2,489	3,011	3,717	4,705	6,146	8,365	12,045	18,821	23,235	29,407
2.1	1,611	2,193	2,610	3,158	3,899	4,935	6,446	8,774	12,635	19,742	24,372	30,846
2.2	1,686	2,295	2,732	3,306	4,081	5,165	6,746	9,182	13,223	20,661	25,507	32,282
2.3	1,761	2,397	2,853	3,452	4,262	5,394	7,046	9,590	13,810	21,578	26,638	33,715
2.4	1,836	2,499	2,974	3,599	4,443	5,623	7,344	9,997	14,395	22,493	27,769	35,145
2.5	1,911	2,600	3,095	3,745	4,623	5,851	7,642	10,403	14,980	23,406	28,896	36,572
2.6	1,985	2,702	3,215	3,891	4,803	6,079	7,940	10,807	15,563	24,317	30,021	37,996
2.7	2,059	2,803	3,336	4,036	4,983	6,307	8,237	11,211	16,145	25,227	31,144	39,416
2.8	2,133	2,904	3,455	4,181	5,162	6,534	8,533	11,615	16,726	26,134	32,264	40,834
2.9	2,207	3,004	3,575	4,326	5,341	6,760	8,829	12,017	17,305	27,039	33,382	42,249
3.0	2,281	3,105	3,695	4,471	5,520	6,986	9,124	12,419	17,884	27,943	34,497	43,661
3.1	2,355	3,205	3,814	4,615	5,697	7,211	9,419	12,820	18,461	28,845	35,611	45,070
3.2	2,428	3,305	3,933	4,759	5,875	7,436	9,712	13,220	19,036	29,745	36,721	46,476
3.3	2,501	3,404	4,051	4,903	6,052	7,660	10,005	13,619	19,611	30,642	37,830	47,878
3.4	2,574	3,504	4,170	5,046	6,229	7,884	10,298	14,017	20,184	31,538	38,936	49,278
3.5	2,647	3,603	4,288	5,189	6,406	8,108	10,590	14,414	20,757	32,432	40,040	50,675
3.6	2,720	3,702	4,406	5,322	6,582	8,331	10,881	14,811	21,328	33,325	41,141	52,069
3.7	2,793	3,801	4,524	5,474	6,758	8,554	11,172	15,207	21,897	34,214	42,240	53,460
3.8	2,865	3,900	4,641	5,616	6,933	8,776	11,462	15,601	22,466	35,103	43,336	54,848
3.9	2,938	3,998	4,759	5,758	7,109	8,997	11,751	15,995	23,033	35,989	44,430	56,233
4.0	3,010	4,097	4,875	5,900	7,283	9,218	12,040	16,388	23,599	36,874	45,522	57,615

Chart 9A.3 Sample Size for Various Percentages of Expected Returns (P) and Limit of Error (E) if Factor of Confidence Is 95 Percent

P	0.50	0.55	0.60	0.65	0.70	0.75	0.80	0.85	0.90	0.95	1.00	1.50
						E						
4.2	6,182	5,109	4,293	3,658	3,154	2,747	2,414	2,139	1,908	1,712	1,545	687
4.4	6,462	5,341	4,488	3,824	3,297	2,872	2,524	2,236	1,994	1,790	1,616	718
4.6	6,742	5,572	4,682	3,989	3,440	2,996	2,633	2,333	2,081	1,867	1,685	749
4.8	7,021	5,802	4,875	4,154	3,582	3,120	2,742	2,429	2,167	1,945	1,755	780
5.0	7,298	6,031	5,068	4,318	3,723	3,243	2,850	2,525	2,252	2,022	1,824	811
5.2	7,574	6,259	5,259	4,481	3,864	3,366	2,958	2,620	2,337	2,098	1,893	841
5.4	7,848	6,486	5,450	4,644	4,004	3,488	3,066	2,716	2,422	2,174	1,962	872
5.6	8,122	6,712	5,640	4,806	4,144	3,609	3,173	2,810	2,506	2,250	2,030	902
5.8	8,394	6,937	5,829	4,967	4,283	3,731	3,279	2,904	2,590	2,325	2,098	933
6.0	8,665	7,161	6,017	5,127	4,421	3,851	3,385	2,998	2,674	2,400	2,166	963

Chart 9A.4 Sample Size for Various
Percentages of Expected Returns (*P*) and Limit
of Error (*E*) if Factor of Confidence Is
95 Percent

| | | | | | | | *E* | | | | | | |
P	2.00	2.50	3.00	3.50	4.00	4.50	5.00	5.50	6.00	6.50	7.00	7.50
4.2	386	247	172	126	96	76	61	51	43	36	31	27
4.4	404	258	179	132	101	80	65	53	45	38	33	28
4.6	421	270	187	138	105	83	67	56	46	40	34	30
4.8	439	281	195	143	109	86	70	58	48	41	36	31
5.0	456	292	202	149	114	90	73	60	50	43	37	32
5.2	473	303	210	154	118	93	76	62	52	45	38	33
5.4	490	314	218	160	123	97	78	65	54	46	40	35
5.6	507	325	225	166	127	100	81	67	56	48	41	36
5.8	524	336	233	171	131	103	84	69	58	50	43	37
6.0	542	346	240	177	135	107	86	71	60	51	44	38

Chart 9A.5 Sample Size for Various Percentages of Expected Returns (P) and Limit of Error (E) if Factor of Confidence Is 99 Percent

P	0.01	0.02	0.03	0.04	0.05	0.06	0.07	0.08	0.09	0.10	0.12	0.14
0.1	662,837	165,709	73,649	41,427	26,513	18,412	13,527	10,357	8,183	6,628	4,603	3,381
0.2	1,324,346	331,087	147,149	82,772	52,974	36,787	27,027	20,693	16,349	13,243	9,197	6,756
0.3	1,984,529	496,132	220,503	124,033	79,381	55,126	40,500	31,008	24,500	19,845	13,781	10,125
0.4	2,643,384	660,846	293,709	165,212	105,735	73,427	53,946	41,303	32,634	26,434	18,356	13,486
0.5	3,300,913	825,228	366,767	206,307	132,037	91,692	67,365	51,577	40,752	33,009	22,923	16,841
0.6	3,957,114	989,279	439,679	247,320	158,285	109,919	80,757	61,830	48,853	39,571	27,480	20,189
0.7	4,611,989	1,152,997	512,443	288,249	184,480	128,111	94,122	72,062	56,938	46,120	32,027	23,530
0.8	5,265,536	1,316,384	585,058	329,096	210,621	146,265	107,459	82,274	65,006	52,655	36,565	26,864
0.9	5,917,757	1,479,439	657,528	369,859	236,710	164,381	120,770	92,465	73,059	59,178	41,095	30,192
1.0	6,568,650	1,642,163	729,850	410,541	262,746	182,463	134,054	102,635	81,094	65,687	45,616	33,513
1.1	7,218,217	1,804,554	802,022	451,138	288,729	200,505	147,310	112,784	89,113	72,182	50,126	36,827
1.2	7,866,456	1,966,614	874,050	491,654	314,658	218,512	160,538	122,913	97,116	78,665	54,628	40,134
1.3	8,513,369	2,128,342	945,929	532,085	340,535	236,482	173,742	133,021	105,102	85,134	59,121	43,435
1.4	9,158,954	2,289,739	1,017,659	572,435	366,358	254,414	186,917	143,108	113,072	91,590	63,603	46,729
1.5	9,803,213	2,450,803	1,089,245	612,700	392,129	272,310	200,065	153,175	121,026	98,032	68,077	50,016
1.6		2,611,536	1,160,682	652,884	417,846	290,170	213,186	163,221	128,964	104,461	72,542	53,296

E

1.7	2,771,937	1,231,970	692,984	443,510	307,992	226,279	173,246	136,885	110,877	76,997	56,569
1.8	2,932,007	1,303,113	733,002	469,121	325,777	239,246	183,250	144,790	117,280	81,444	59,836
1.9	3,091,744	1,374,109	772,936	494,679	343,527	252,385	193,234	152,679	123,670	85,881	63,096
2.0	3,251,150	1,444,952	812,788	520,184	361,238	265,400	203,197	160,549	130,046	90,309	66,350
2.1	3,410,224	1,515,654	852,556	545,636	378,912	278,385	213,139	168,405	136,409	94,728	69,596
2.2	3,568,967	1,586,207	892,242	571,035	396,551	291,344	223,060	176,244	142,759	99,138	72,836
2.3	3,727,377	1,656,608	931,844	596,380	414,152	304,274	232,961	184,095	149,095	103,537	76,068
2.4	3,885,456	1,726,868	971,364	621,673	431,716	317,178	242,841	191,874	155,418	107,929	79,294
2.5	4,043,203	1,796,979	1,010,800	646,913	449,245	330,055	252,700	199,664	161,728	112,311	82,513
2.6	4,200,619	1,866,938	1,050,155	672,099	466,734	342,905	262,538	207,437	168,025	116,682	85,726
2.7	4,357,702	1,936,755	1,089,425	697,232	484,187	355,730	272,356	215,195	174,308	121,046	88,932
2.8	4,514,454	2,006,424	1,128,614	722,313	501,606	368,526	282,153	222,936	180,578	125,402	92,131
2.9	4,670,874	2,075,940	1,167,718	747,340	518,984	381,295	291,929	230,658	186,835	129,745	95,324
3.0	4,826,963	2,145,314	1,206,741	772,314	536,327	394,036	301,685	238,366	193,079	134,081	98,508
3.1	4,982,719	2,214,541	1,245,679	797,235	553,635	406,751	311,420	246,058	199,309	138,409	101,687
3.2	5,138,144	2,283,614	1,284,536	822,103	570,903	419,438	321,134	253,734	205,526	142,725	104,858
3.3	5,293,237	2,352,547	1,323,309	846,918	588,135	432,098	330,827	261,393	211,729	147,034	108,024
3.4	5,447,999	2,421,332	1,362,000	871,680	605,333	444,734	340,500	269,036	217,920	151,333	111,183
3.5	5,602,428	2,489,963	1,400,607	896,389	622,490	457,341	350,152	276,662	224,097	155,621	114,334
3.6	5,756,526	2,558,453	1,439,132	921,044	639,611	469,919	359,783	284,273	230,261	159,903	117,479
3.7	5,910,292	2,626,797	1,477,573	945,647	656,699	482,471	369,393	291,866	236,412	164,174	120,616
3.8	6,063,727	2,694,984	1,515,932	970,196	673,746	494,996	378,983	299,440	242,549	168,435	123,749
3.9	6,216,829	2,763,032	1,554,207	994,693	690,756	507,493	388,552	307,001	248,673	172,688	126,872
4.0	6,369,600	2,830,933	1,592,400	1,019,136	707,733	519,964	398,100	314,546	254,784	176,933	129,991

Chart 9A.6 Sample Size for Various Percentages of Expected Returns (P) and Limit of Error (E) if Factor of Confidence Is 99 Percent

P	0.16	0.18	0.20	0.25	0.30	0.35	0.40	0.45	0.50	0.55	0.60	0.70
0.1	2,589	2,046	1,657	1,060	736	541	414	327	265	219	184	135
0.2	5,173	4,087	3,311	2,119	1,471	1,081	827	654	529	437	368	270
0.3	7,752	6,125	4,961	3,175	2,205	1,620	1,240	980	794	656	551	405
0.4	10,325	8,158	6,608	4,229	2,937	2,158	1,652	1,305	1,057	874	734	539
0.5	12,894	10,187	8,252	5,281	3,667	2,694	2,063	1,630	1,320	1,091	916	673
0.6	15,457	12,213	9,893	6,331	4,396	3,230	2,473	1,954	1,582	1,308	1,099	807
0.7	18,015	14,234	11,530	7,379	5,124	3,765	2,882	2,277	1,845	1,524	1,218	941
0.8	20,569	16,251	13,164	8,424	5,850	4,298	3,291	2,600	2,106	1,740	1,462	1,074
0.9	23,116	18,264	14,794	9,468	6,575	4,830	3,698	2,922	2,367	1,956	1,643	1,208
1.0	25,658	20,273	16,422	10,510	7,299	5,362	4,105	3,243	2,627	2,171	1,825	1,340
1.1	28,195	22,278	18,045	11,549	8,020	5,892	4,511	3,564	2,887	2,386	2,004	1,473
1.2	30,728	24,279	19,666	12,586	8,740	6,421	4,917	3,884	3,146	2,600	2,185	1,605
1.3	33,255	26,275	21,283	13,621	9,459	6,949	5,321	4,204	3,405	2,814	2,365	1,737
1.4	35,777	28,268	22,897	14,654	10,176	7,476	5,724	4,522	3,663	3,028	2,544	1,869
1.5	38,293	30,256	24,508	15,685	10,892	8,002	6,127	4,841	3,921	3,241	2,723	2,000
1.6	40,805	32,241	26,115	16,714	11,607	8,527	6,529	5,158	4,178	3,453	2,901	2,132

E

1.7	43,311	34,221	27,719	17,740	12,319	9,051	6,930	5,475	4,435	3,665	3,079	2,263
1.8	45,812	36,197	29,320	18,764	13,030	9,574	7,330	5,791	4,691	3,877	3,257	2,393
1.9	48,308	38,169	30,917	19,787	13,741	10,095	7,729	6,107	4,946	4,088	3,435	2,523
2.0	50,799	40,137	32,512	20,807	14,449	10,616	8,128	6,421	5,202	4,299	3,612	2,654
2.1	53,284	42,100	34,102	21,825	15,156	11,135	8,525	6,736	5,456	4,509	3,789	2,783
2.2	55,765	44,061	35,690	22,841	15,862	11,653	8,922	7,050	5,710	4,719	3,965	2,913
2.3	58,239	46,016	37,273	23,855	16,566	12,171	9,318	7,362	5,964	4,928	4,141	3,042
2.4	60,710	47,968	38,855	24,867	17,268	12,687	9,714	7,674	6,216	5,137	4,317	3,172
2.5	63,174	49,915	40,432	25,877	17,970	13,202	10,108	7,986	6,469	5,346	4,492	3,300
2.6	65,634	51,859	42,006	26,884	18,669	13,716	10,501	8,297	6,721	5,554	4,667	3,429
2.7	68,088	53,798	43,577	27,889	19,367	14,229	10,894	8,608	6,972	5,762	4,842	3,557
2.8	70,538	55,734	45,145	28,892	20,064	14,740	11,286	8,917	7,223	5,969	5,016	3,685
2.9	72,982	57,664	46,708	29,893	20,759	15,251	11,677	9,226	7,473	6,176	5,189	3,812
3.0	75,421	59,591	48,270	30,893	21,453	15,761	12,067	9,534	7,723	6,382	5,363	3,940
3.1	77,854	61,514	49,827	31,889	22,145	16,270	12,457	9,842	7,972	6,589	5,536	4,067
3.2	80,284	63,433	51,381	32,884	22,836	16,777	12,845	10,149	8,221	6,794	5,709	4,194
3.3	82,706	65,348	52,932	33,876	23,525	17,284	13,233	10,455	8,469	6,999	5,881	4,321
3.4	85,124	67,258	54,480	34,867	24,213	17,789	13,620	10,761	8,716	7,204	6,053	4,447
3.5	87,537	69,165	56,024	35,856	24,899	18,293	14,006	11,066	8,964	7,408	6,224	4,573
3.6	89,945	71,067	57,565	36,842	25,584	18,796	14,391	11,370	9,210	7,612	6,395	4,699
3.7	92,347	72,966	59,103	37,825	26,268	19,299	14,775	11,370	9,456	7,815	6,567	4,824
3.8	94,745	74,860	60,637	38,807	26,949	19,799	15,159	11,977	9,702	8,018	6,737	4,949
3.9	97,137	76,750	62,168	39,787	27,629	20,299	15,542	12,279	9,947	8,220	6,907	5,074
4.0	99,525	78,636	63,696	40,765	28,309	20,798	15,924	12,581	10,191	8,422	7,077	5,199

Chart 9A.7 Sample Size for Various Percentages of Expected Returns (P) and Limit of Error (E) if Factor of Confidence Is 99 Percent

P	E											
	0.50	0.55	0.60	0.65	0.70	0.75	0.80	0.85	0.90	0.95	1.00	1.50
4.2	10,678	8,825	7,415	6,319	5,448	4,745	4,171	3,694	3,296	2,958	2,669	1,186
4.4	11,163	9,225	7,752	6,605	5,695	4,961	4,361	3,862	3,445	3,092	2,791	1,240
4.6	11,646	9,625	8,088	6,891	5,942	5,176	4,549	4,029	3,594	3,226	2,911	1,294
4.8	12,127	10,023	8,421	7,176	6,187	5,390	4,737	4,196	3,743	3,359	3,032	1,347
5.0	12,607	10,418	8,754	7,459	6,431	5,603	4,924	4,362	3,890	3,492	3,152	1,401
5.2	13,083	10,812	9,085	7,741	6,674	5,814	5,110	4,526	4,037	3,623	3,270	1,453
5.4	13,557	11,205	9,414	8,022	6,917	6,025	5,295	4,691	4,184	3,755	3,389	1,506
5.6	14,030	11,595	9,743	8,302	7,158	6,235	5,481	4,854	4,329	3,886	3,507	1,559
5.8	14,500	11,983	10,069	8,580	7,398	6,445	5,664	5,017	4,475	4,016	3,625	1,611
6.0	14,969	12,370	10,394	8,856	7,636	6,652	5,847	5,179	4,619	4,146	3,742	1,663

Chart 9A.8 Sample Size for Various Percentages of Expected Returns (P) and Limit of Error (E) if Factor of Confidence Is 99 Percent

						E						
P	2.00	2.50	3.00	3.50	4.00	4.50	5.00	5.50	6.00	6.50	7.00	7.50
4.2	667	427	297	218	167	131	106	88	74	63	54	47
4.4	697	447	310	228	174	137	111	92	77	66	56	49
4.6	728	466	323	238	182	143	116	96	80	68	59	52
4.8	758	485	336	247	189	149	121	100	84	72	62	54
5.0	788	504	350	257	196	155	126	104	87	74	64	56
5.2	817	523	363	267	204	161	131	107	90	77	66	58
5.4	847	542	376	276	212	167	135	111	94	80	69	60
5.6	876	561	389	286	219	173	140	115	97	83	71	62
5.8	906	580	403	295	226	178	145	119	100	86	74	64
6.0	936	598	415	305	234	184	149	123	104	88	76	66

CHAPTER 10

Internal Files: A Hidden Asset

THE VALUE OF A LIST

There is no doubt from any point of view that a list has value—excellent value. That's a given. The capitalized value? That's a problem. The evaluation formula? There isn't any. The list has no intrinsic value since it can't be capitalized and/or depreciated. Simplistically, the customer list is an intangible asset inseparable from the goodwill and operation of the business.

But isn't it inconceivable that a mail-order business, a magazine, book, or record club being offered for sale could be sold separate and apart from its customer list? The list must be considered an integral part of the purchase of the specific business as a whole. If, as it has been reported, the rule of thumb for buyouts of mail-order firms is 13 times earnings, where would the earning come from without a customer file?

WHAT IS THE MAILING LIST?

To a:

List broker, it's a client and prospect file and its product.

List compiler, it's a product.

Catalog or merchandise company, it's a customer file.

Magazine, it's a subscriber file.

Record or book club, it's a membership file.

Fundraiser, it's a donor file.

Association, it's a membership file.

Club, it's a membership file.

Doesn't this immediately point out the problem of determining by an overall formula the basis for establishing the value of a list? Each situation has its own dynamics.

GOODWILL

When selling or buying a business, one aspect which may represent a large portion of the price is goodwill. *Goodwill* is principally the intangible asset of a business such as the customer base, customer list, reputation, and history—in other words, the prestige that a business has acquired beyond the mere value of what it sells. Goodwill encompasses any elements that contribute to the worth of a business but are not included in financial statements. Goodwill is treated as a capital asset, and the seller treats it as capital gain. However, the purchaser of the company cannot deduct the cost of the goodwill. The purchaser gets the money back only when and if the business is sold.

How to value goodwill is not a straightforward process in any business, but establishing the value of a list is harder to deal with than most. Simplistically, we might say that goodwill represents those factors that make customers remain as customers, which results in profits or return on investment that could not be generated solely from the assets listed on the balance sheet.

In discussing, over the years, the methodology which could be used to work up a formula for establishing the worth of a name, the conclusion is that there is no magic formula. In pragmatic terms, the best approach to value measurement appears to be the development of a menu of particulars which need to be considered in *list value creation* (LVC).

Virtually every decision regarding any business strategy is based on

management assumptions. Creating the LVC is no exception. But before assumptions can be applied, you need a starting point—historical data going back 2 to 3 years based on:

1. **Quantitative analysis.** This involves numbers, e.g., quantity of names, response rates, sales, list rental income, historical bad debts, or credit standing of customer groupings.
2. **Qualitative analysis.** This type of analysis evaluates the nonnumerical aspects of the list, e.g., source of names, competition, customer geographical distribution, or quality of product or service.

From this exercise you can develop an LVC form which includes the historical data plus the assumptions which must be used to come up with the appraised value, a good figure to know whether or not this becomes a balance sheet item. Send the document to your management, marketing, and financial teams requesting input on the assumptions.

Tabulate the results. Should major discrepancies surface, discuss and determine the reasons. This could result in a workable and effective valuation procedure.

LET'S START THE MENU

There are two basic sales conditions:

1. Selling the entire business
2. Selling the list separately because operations will cease
   a. To a competitive company
   b. To a noncompetitive company

The type of business or list being sold is another factor, for example, a magazine, book, or record club and merchandise (catalogs).

SELLING THE LIST SEPARATELY

Let's start with an infrequent occurrence: someone buying the list of a defunct company only for income from rentals. In this instance the purchase price must be calculated on the potential number of rentals based on: the type of list, the age of the names, the unit of sale, and the previous rental history.

In reviewing the previous list rental history, make a determination of:

1. Number of tests versus continuations to get an indication of the responsiveness of the list

2. Whether or not the list had been promoted to all possible markets including competitors (Secure information on the number of competitive companies. The probability of market expansion is a key factor in projecting list rental income.)

Both of these points are critical because the lifespan of a list which will not be updated is short. Considering population mobility, it is obvious that deliverability would be a problem and would unfavorably impact on response. What is the life span of a list offered for outright sale for list rental purposes only? An arbitrary standard would be 1 to 1½ years.

SELLING THE LIST TO A COMPETITIVE FIRM

On the other hand, if a company were being dissolved and its various assets being sold separately, the list could then be offered on its own merit. In this instance, a competitive company might wish to pay a premium for the names as a means of adding a qualified audience to its own house list.

Here are some general key factors which need to be quantified and qualified:

1. Description of product or service
2. List size
3. Sources used to build the list
4. Unit of sale
5. Age of names (recency)
6. List exchanges, if any and with which companies (invaluable in assessing the competition and/or the marketplace)
7. If list was available for rental, the number of tests and continuations as an indicator of success ratio
8. For the company purchasing the list, the relationship of the demographics and psychographics to the purchaser's product(s)
9. Societal trends (Does the list under scrutiny represent an audience which can be defined as being in a growing population segment? Or is it in a declining socioeconomic group?)
10. Quality of list maintenance including order entry, address changes, payments, source, dollar value of customer—in other words, the capture of purchasing behavior elements leading to a customer profile
11. Quality of the product(s) or service(s) sold relative to competitive products or services *and* the acquiring company's products or services
12. For the company purchasing the list, an evaluation of previous re-

sponse history (For example, the purchaser uses list A with a 1 percent response, and the seller uses list A with a 2 percent response. Does this mean that the seller has a stronger marketing approach, a better product or service? Or was it only the lower price which attracted a different audience?)

13. List rental income with a detail of expenses charged against income (overhead, processing and billing charges, etc.)
14. The extent to which ancillary products or services were promoted successfully
15. The extent to which former buyers and expires respond to the company's promotions

Some of these descriptors have more value than others and should be so weighted. There is no formula for this either. It depends specifically on the business plan drawn up by the purchaser which outlines the reasons for the purchase and the expectations.

Not so incidentally, some of these points also relate to the dollar valuation of internal files because, generally, in most businesses, various methods exist for computing goodwill based on *earning power*. Those are the key words. *Caveat*: The value of earning power cannot be confirmed by referring to objective evidence. It is subject to constant change due to internal, external, and other spirals of influence on earnings.

LIST VALUE CREATION

In the selling of companies in the service industries (publishers, insurance companies, stock brokers, and others), the purchase of the customer list is, without equivocation, an important part of the deal. But most often the customer list is included under goodwill. Let's forget (if we can) goodwill for the moment. Let's think of all direct marketers, regardless of the business they're in, as service industries. And also let's assume that the customer list can be capitalized. (Forget the sale of the business.)

Would it be reasonable to try to establish the dollar value of each name on the file by means of a justifiable calculation? Wouldn't the worth of a name lead to the list value creation (LVC)? For example, you're in the catalog business, and you want to find the dollar value of the accounts on the customer list. You might find the average billing for a good customer and multiply it by the frequency rate. You would then discount it by the turnover rate for this type of customer, perhaps, let's say, 30 percent.

And let's go a step further. Perhaps the popular 80-20 principle of inventory applies to customers. (In most companies 20 percent of inventory items make up 80 percent of inventory value.) It is these customers

representing the upper quintile who should be given a higher score and it is these customers who should be studied to determine the rate of turn-over and the cost to replace them as high-value customers. The size of a list is an important factor, but only if evaluated properly. Average unit of sale is not the determinant—the average can be unduly influenced by a group of customers at the high end and a group of customers at the low end. The size of each of these subgroups is an important ingredient.

Recognize that no formula can be "all things to all companies." In addition to list size and other general factors discussed previously, let's look at some specifics by line of business which should be scrutinized for list value creation.

Specific Factors Applying to Magazines

1. Length of time subscribers have been on the file (i.e., 1 year, 2 years, over 3 years)
2. Renewal rate based on length of time on file and offer on which they were acquired
3. *Source*: solo direct mail, subscription agency, radio, TV, space, inserts (valuation based on persistency by source versus cost)
4. *Offer*: full rate, trial, discount offer, sweeps, premiums, complimentary copy (valuation based on cost per order and persistency)
5. Income from subscriber
6. Value of expires to the magazine as a source of new subscribers (expires can pull 30 to 50 percent better than outside lists in some instances); total number of names used for in-house promotion (Also calculate the value for other magazines, books, or services offered by the company)
7. Credit/collection history
8. List rental income and how this income is accounted for and what expenses are charged to this income stream
9. Promotion expenses involving the cost of securing subscribers

Specific Factors Applying to Book and Record Clubs

1. Average lifetime of member based on offer and source or any other measurement unit which makes sense
2. *Offer*: commitment versus no commitment, free books, etc.
3. How many members satisfy the commitment and stop
4. What percentage of members continue to purchase after the commitment has been satisfied
5. Average income per member (lifetime value)
6. Status of accounts (gross sales, returns, and nonpay per member)

7. Review credit "conditions" to determine accounts receivable and collection history
8. List rental income

Specific Factors Applying to Merchandise Lists

1. *Source*
   a. Direct mail
   b. Other sources (space, TV and/or broadcast, mixed media, telephone)
   c. Direct sale versus two-step process (i.e., space inquiry to buyer)
2. *Buyers' file mix, recency:*
   Month, quarter, 6 months, year
3. *Attrition rate*
4. *Customer purchasing behavior*
   a. Average sale by year or any other measurement time frame
   b. Cash, credit card, bill me (Evaluate average sale by each payment mode.)
   c. Percent male versus female
   d. A description of the most popular items sold (to add another coordinate to the customer profile)
5. *Response from internal files versus rental lists (sales and cost)*
6. *List rental income*

COST-TO-CREATE METHOD

In the November 1984 issue of *The Business Owner* magazine (383 South Broadway, Hicksville, New York) the cost-to-create method was discussed:

> This bases the value of an intangible asset on the cost required to duplicate it. For example, suppose a company has developed a mailing list, with the cost to do so having already been incurred and expensed. Thus, it will carry no value on the company's balance sheet.
>
> Its value, using this method, would be calculated as follows:

Labor	$30,000
Materials	10,000
Management time	15,000
Outside professional services	13,000
Subtotal	$68,000
Return on investment: Assumed at 12 percent	8,160
Total cost to create	$76,160

The first step is to identify all costs associated with developing (or producing) the intangible asset. In this case, it was a mailing list. Other examples are product catalogs, customer lists, and a production process. After the costs are identified, you can apply a return factor on the money used to develop the asset.

Keep in mind that the $76,160 total value is in addition to the company's reported net worth (stockholder's equity). Reason: The costs for developing the mailing list were previously expensed.

NO MAGIC FORMULA

While no definitive methodology or magic formula exists, the direction is quite clear. Each company must define the discrete items to be included in the LVC format. By observing some important guidelines and avoiding some common pitfalls, you'll find the path to the LVC will be smoothed out considerably. It will be a provocative and useful exercise which could make it possible to do a P&L on definitive groups of names from the historical data. When this is accomplished, you would have a reasonably accurate evaluation of your house list—the hidden asset.

Waves of Change

One of the most important factors in all the measurement and analytical disciplines is *trend analysis*, that is, the understanding of the socioeconomic trends which have influenced the marketplace dramatically in recent years. It is even more important to recognize that these socioeconomic trends will continue at a rapid pace because of the compelling effect of modern science on our society. The ability to adapt to a swifter changing scene is a *must* for every company's future.

You can neither fight nor ignore "market winds." The market is a dynamic force and must be watched as closely as the river that is threatening to overflow its banks or the tornado warning that requires certain protective measures to be taken. As an example, in the early 1900s there were about 125 carriage companies. The owners were hearing about a noisy, odorous contraption that could transport people without horse or donkey power. Most of the owners decided that there was no way that the horse-drawn carriage could be replaced by this new invention. After all, this mode of transportation had been in use for thousands of years. Two companies, however, decided that they were not in the carriage business but in the transportation business. One became Ford, the other General Motors. Observing and projecting the market winds is an essential part of analysis and planning.

Actually, markets are rarely precisely defined. In a changing societal environment, changes can be easily obscured if trends are not studied and observed. We can no longer think of consumers as unitarian and monolithic (see Chart 11.1).

Chart 11.1   Societal Trends: Creating Tomorrow's Customers and Products

Working Women: Socioeconomic Force

1. Half the labor force.
2. More than half of all married women work.
3. By 1990, only one out of four married women will be a full-time housewife.

Families (Preliminary Report from Census 1970–1980)

1. Two-career couples.
2. Total number of households increased from 63.4 to 80.4 million.
3. America in solitary.
4. Fast-growing family type—households maintained by women—increased by 51 percent versus 11 percent growth in families. Families maintained by a man increased by 33.6 percent.
5. 20 percent of children reside with only one parent.
6. Consumer buying unit.

Age Distribution of the Population

1. Majority of U.S. population (as a result of baby boom between 1946 and 1954) represents about 53.4 million.
2. 45 to 54 market represents 25 percent of spending in United States; over-45 group represents the largest pool of *purchasing power* to impact on U.S. economy.
3. 55 to 64 age group represents about 20 percent of all discretionary income.
4. The mature market comes of age.

Geographical Shifts (Where of the Market)

1. Life on the fringes.
2. Amenity-rich areas.
3. Gentrification.
4. Change of address.

Recreation, Home Entertainment Center

1. Marriage of home computer and communication.
2. Electronic recreation room.
3. Products and services for use in the home offer new product opportunities.
4. Recreation outside the home—travel, outdoor activities.

THIS IS THE AGE OF THE INDIVIDUAL

When we think of trends, we must think in terms of *people*. It's not so much that there are more of us as that we're more diverse. There is individuality today, and what we see are people with different attitudes, different preferences, different lifestyles. People no longer can be counted on for acting exactly the same way because they are clustered in similar geographic and demographic environments. Demography is still a valid measurement, but we need to add some new dimensions.

The consumer is displaying purchasing trends from quantity to quality, from abundance toward sufficiency, and from spendthrift toward directed spending, and he or she is emphasizing comfort, value, time-saving, fun, nostalgia, beauty, safety, escape, and naturalism.

SOME OF THE CHANGES

The 1980 Census traced two trends that have most affected the picture of America: (1) the post-World War II baby boom, which is working its way through the 25 to 40 age bracket with its own set of values and (2) the fastest-growing segment of U.S. society, which represents the older folks aged 55 and beyond.

Let's look at how these major population shifts have led to dispersed markets.

Married and Single

It's no statistical secret that many "single" people today are living "married" lives and vice versa. For instance, almost half the labor force today is female, and more than half of all "married" women now work outside the home. By the end of this decade, perhaps only one wife in four will be a full-time homemaker. This make a big difference in our mental picture of the "typical married woman." Actually, the women's market is where all the growth has been in the last decade.

Statistically, the number of "single men" in our population has been growing. But we can't presume that we're talking about an equal market growth in carefree bachelors. Demonstrably, many "single" men are living "married" lives; and the women they live with, in or out of wedlock, are probably holding down jobs, which gets us into a "share-the-chores" situation: both sexes involved in cooking, marketing, and child care. There is already a recognition of this new trend, as discussed in a book entitled *Mingles: A Home-Buying Guide for Unmarried Couples* by Robert Irwin, published by McGraw-Hill Book Company. In our penchant for labeling, "mingles" must be the term for couples living together in unwedded bliss.

Households Headed by Women and/or Men

Households headed by women were the fastest-growing family type in the 1980s. American families grew by 12 percent, but households maintained by women increased 51 percent to 8,500,000. This relative dissolution of the traditional family was caused by separation, divorce, widowhood, and the ability of women to establish independent families. Families maintained by a man without a wife increased by 33.6 percent. Twenty percent of children under 18 (one out of five) reside with only one parent according to the Census Bureau, indicating that divorce continues to be a major phenomenon in American society. This was an increase of 53.9 percent since 1970.

In looking at these changes it is obvious that traditional presumptions are no longer safe. It is a complex marketplace today, and, for instance, if you use the traditional targeting aimed at women, you're missing the huge audience of husbands and/or men living alone. And conversely, many traditionally male-oriented products such as financial and travel services or cars and liquor are at last being targeted to women. If you accept the premise demographers advance that the "household" be regarded as a "consumer buying unit," would you not consider the idea of gender-neutral terminology?

Time Moves On

Can the shifts in the age distribution of the population be ignored? Older consumers comprise one of the hottest up-and-coming markets in the nation. Businesses must look to the fact that people over 50, the "maturity" market, are about 26 percent of the population and increasing. The famous 18 to 34 market now targeted by Madison Avenue will, over the next several decades, be equaled or outstripped by the over-45 market. (It's nice to know that there is a life after 34!) Even today, those over 45s control 60 percent of all discretionary income, and, if it's over 50, 50.2 percent of discretionary income. They can buy what they want—not just what they need. No advertiser can ignore a market of consumers aged 55 and over with an estimated $300 billion buying potential.

Does this not suggest that we're moving toward an "age-irrelevant" society based on psychographics? Doesn't it also suggest that to lump together all the over-50s is too broad a segmentation? The 50 to 64s comprise one out of every five adults and will increase in the next decade. Marketers must consider this significant and vital consumer sector with product development imagination which addresses an active, affluent lifestyle and not just the stereotypical "rocking-chair" approach. The trend has already begun toward a class-market development in publications, products, and advertising aimed at the older consumer.

Many of these societal winds have produced the dawn of a new segment—the affluent market, a market that has already reshaped marketing. Estimates vary on the income necessary to join this elite group; while the $40,000 to $50,000 income levels are common thresholds, some researchers consider them too low.

Much depends, it would seem, on family composition and education. Single-person households, for example, have fewer fixed expenditures and a higher proportion of discretionary income than husband-wife households with similar incomes. Some observers feel that a relationship does exist between education and income. True, but while a rich electrician may not have the educational level of a rich executive, this disparity does not affect purchasing *power*—but it could affect purchasing behavior. Affluence is more than just dollars and cents. It is an increasingly heterogeneous group of people with their own lifestyle and consumption patterns.

The superaffluent market ($50,000+) will grow as a result of the baby-boomers growing into their most productive years, two-income families and the middle-aged affluentials.

In summary, bear in mind that in every segment there are gradations. Generic names for "demographic" groups such as Yuppies (*young urban professionals*), Yumps (*young upwardly mobile population*), and Yaps (*young aspiring professionals*) do not tell the whole story. Then there are the Lumps (*life-giving, unselfish, middle-class, parent, survivors*) from the mature segment, who spawned the Yuppies, etc. Even before these cute descriptors disappear, the gradations within these labels must be recognized.

WHERE DO THEY ALL LIVE?

The *where* of our market must be considered. Demographically, we used to profile in categories such as urban, suburban, and rural, and we presumed the homogeneity of lifestyle within our given neighborhood. But the currents of change have been shifting our targets, often scattering them.

The way we live today has been completely reshaped by the jet plane, sophisticated telephonic communications, and the virtually instant data transmission facilities now available to business. Corporations that once clustered in major cities out of necessity are now scattered throughout the country. The business-to-business marketer no longer has to settle where the customers are because these customers are now so far-flung that it is impossible to set up where they are. Urban populations are thinning; office buildings and research centers are springing up in the older suburbs. What used to be the distant exurbs are the growing residential areas, and the census tract or Zip code area that used to be rural now has executive homes where barns and pastures once were.

Some states are struggling with industrial decline while others try to cope with the problems of industrial growth. Yesterday, the "sunbelt" states were booming. Tomorrow, sunbelt inflation and "frostbelt" recession may persuade the maturity market that their dollars will buy more in the cold-weather states.

EARNING A LIVING

Think about another phenomenon: There has been a noticeable change in the way people earn their living. About 3 decades ago approximately 51 percent of the population worked in agriculture, commerce, and manufacturing. Today only about 28 percent of the working population is employed in these areas. The typical worker today creates, processes, and disseminates information. By 1990, according to one estimate, 80 percent of American homes will have small computers. While this figure may be high, even half would be important for the future. This may be why it is being predicted that the minicomputer and microcomputer, which are getting increased power while they are getting smaller and unit prices are falling, will hasten the shift to decentralized work locations for 20 percent of the work force in this decade. It is estimated that 50 percent of the 106 million or so workers in the United States are involved in information-related jobs. These types of jobs will enable some to work at home and thus will increase participation of homeworkers and disabled individuals in the work force. Being able to work at home will influence choice of residences by employees, and business will benefit from reduced real estate costs due to smaller office size. Think about how this employment shift will impact geographics.

ELECTRONIC ROOM

In the home, the marriage of computers and communications will impact forever the way Americans spend their time. Nonproductive repetitive tasks such as commuting, shopping, and paying bills will decrease as hours spent on work at home, education, and leisure will increase. Think of the futuristic visions of compose-it-yourself magazines, newspapers, and specialty catalogs, all of which made possible by your personal computer which allows access to special-interest information out of some distant data base.

RECOGNIZING TRENDS AND THINKING AHEAD

These new economical, technological, and societal developments must not be ignored because they are the marketing strategists' key to the future.

People *are* different. It's already not the way it was and not the way it's going to be. People are going to be in different numbers, in different ages with different interests—more selective and more conservative. The sharp marketer will need to address these variances. Therefore, we can expect a trend away from mass-produced goods and a flourishing of individualized goods and services.

IMPACT OF SOCIETAL CHANGES ON LIST TRENDS

In relating list trends to societal forces (Appendix 11A), it is interesting to note the following:

The universe for business and finance increased by 61.8 percent. This average was dramatically impacted by the increase in investment services, credit cards, and women in business and careers.

New technology increased by 123.4 percent, which confirms the interest in personal computers as well as technology on every front.

Hobbies and special interest increased by 21 percent. Female "how-to" reflects the trend toward the home as does the men's how-to. Out of a relatively static housing industry (an economical trend) and a strong automobile aftermarket emerged a strong do-it-yourself market, estimated at $100 billion by 1988. Do-it-yourselfers can save from 50 to 60 percent on costs, and also get a feeling of pride. It's more of a hobby now than a task.

Entertainment represents a $244 billion market in the United States with money spent in pursuit of leisure accounting for about $1 in every $8 spent by American consumers. These figures support the recreational societal trends previously mentioned.

Reading, while the universe is still substantial, does show a small increase overall.

The personal interests category dramatizes the "feeling-good" revolution in the United States. The interest in health extends to science, physical well-being, enhancement of lifestyle, feeling good, keeping fit, healthy relationships, growing up, getting older, and reducing stress—which altogether make up a health management program. This category also reflects the aging of the population.

The home interest and/or family category is self-explanatory. The purchase of merchandise by mail is dramatic with over 117,881,000 names. If you add to this figure women's and men's personal merchandise, the total is 182,578,000 names (not accounting for duplication). This has been influenced by the number of women in the work force and the convenience of shopping by mail.

The 95.5 percent increase in the fund raising list market can be traced to the higher level of earnings and an increase in social consciousness.

THE ONLY CONSTANT IS CHANGE

In our ever-changing society, trends continue to shift as do consumer attitudes, values, and lifestyles. No program can fully anticipate the caprices of demography, psychography, or the economy, but for the enlightened marketer, the systematic flow of information is at the very core of the marketing concept. It provides the vital link between the relevant environment and the company's marketplace and management intuition.

To borrow on Plato's observation that "education never stops. It's cumulative," in direct mail, information never stops. It's cumulative.

APPENDIX 11A

Impact of Societal Changes on List Trends

Chart 11A.1 Business and Finance

	1984		1983		Percent Change	
	No. of Lists	(000) Universe	No. of Lists	(000) Universe	No. of Lists	Universe
General business reading; business and career improvement	245	56,494	251	52,743	(2.4)	7.1
Investment services	419	33,141	356	23,610	17.7	40.4
Credit card; business T&E	36	68,333	26	16,525	38.5	313.5
Family money management and consumer rating books and magazines	26	9,337	23	9,193	13.0	1.6
Women in business and careers	75	13,572	78	9,740	(3.8)	39.3
Total	801	180,877	734	111,811	9.1	61.8

Chart 11A.2   New Technology

	1984		1983		Percent Change	
	No. of Lists	(000) Universe	No. of Lists	(000) Universe	No. of Lists	Universe
New technology	283	21,170	163	9478	73.6	123.4

Chart 11A.3   Hobbies and Special Interests

	1984		1983		Percent Change	
	No. of Lists	(000) Universe	No. of Lists	(000) Universe	No. of Lists	Universe
Special-interest reading	19	2,342	22	2,131	(13.6)	9.9
Female-oriented how-to: includes cookbooks, recipe cards, sewing, etc.	125	27,354	120	22,310	4.2	22.6
Sports, outdoors, camping, boating, horses	378	60,583	349	46,314	8.3	30.8
Automotive and motorcycles	76	25,662	74	18,067	2.7	42.0
Photography (professional and amateur)	58	11,109	56	9,780	3.6	13.6
Men's reading	18	5,591	19	5,748	(5.3)	(2.7)
Men's how-to, men's hobbies and interests, electronics	126	23,698	120	21,164	5.0	12.0
Gardening	73	22,155	77	19,809	(5.2)	11.8
Collectibles, antiques, antique reproductions, art collectors	131	11,067	133	11,293	(1.5)	(2.0)
Total	1004	189,561	970	156,616	3.5	21.0

Chart 11A.4   Entertainment

	1984		1983		Percent Change	
	No. of Lists	(000) Universe	No. of Lists	(000) Universe	No. of Lists	Universe
Records and tapes	43	19,764	39	16,149	10.3	22.4
Music and stereo (includes publications and merchandise)	29	4,086	24	2,498	20.8	63.6
Gourmet foods; gourmet cooking	100	20,079	85	15,672	17.6	28.1
Travel	49	12,117	38	4,934	28.9	145.6
Entertainment (theater, concerts, dance, opera, movies, home video, etc.)	132	23,081	135	13,637	(2.2)	69.3
Games and intellectual recreation	15	1,369	13	1,039	15.4	31.8
Total	368	80,496	334	53,929	10.2	49.3

Chart 11A.5   Reading

	1984		1983		Percent Change	
	No. of Lists	(000) Universe	No. of Lists	(000) Universe	No. of Lists	Universe
General and cultural	91	30,147	100	29,285	(9.0)	2.9
Nature and science	48	5,991	50	6,032	(4.0)	(0.7)
Art	40	4,221	44	3,922	(9.1)	7.6
History and military	35	3,309	37	3,460	(5.4)	(4.4)
News and politics	54	13,093	56	14,113	(3.6)	(7.2)
Regionals	123	7,888	131	8,118	(6.1)	(2.8)
Escapist (includes science fiction, mystery, humor)	29	4,931	19	3,491	52.6	41.2
Total	420	69,580	437	68,421	(3.9)	1.7

Chart 11A.6   Personal Pursuits

	1984		1983		Percent Change	
	No. of Lists	(000) Universe	No. of Lists	(000) Universe	No. of Lists	Universe
Opportunity seekers	169	43,309	185	35,532	(8.6)	21.9
Health and fitness	178	38,602	175	28,048	1.7	37.6
Insurance and senior citizen	52	78,059	43	45,830	20.9	70.3
Religious, ethnic	125	31,921	125	77,224	—	(58.7)
Occult; metaphysical; astrology	27	9,460	26	9,474	3.8	(0.1)
Total	551	201,351	554	196,108	(0.5)	2.7

Chart 11A.7   Home Interest, Family, Merchandise

	1984		1983		Percent Change	
	No. of Lists	(000) Universe	No. of Lists	(000) Universe	No. of Lists	Universe
Consumer catalog; general merchandise	266	117,881	262	94,058	1.5	25.3
Parents, children, families, students	242	88,394	207	66,967	16.9	32.0
Women's personal merchandise (cosmetics, apparel, jewelry, etc.)	213	56,684	191	54,142	11.5	4.7
Shelter magazines and women's reading	51	39,009	49	32,393	4.1	20.4
Men's personal merchandise (apparel, jewelry, smoking accessories, etc.)	61	8,013	60	7,793	1.7	2.8
Total	833	309,981	769	255,353	8.3	21.4

Chart 11A.8 Fund Raising

	1984		1983		Percent Change	
	No. of Lists	(000) Universe	No. of Lists	(000) Universe	No. of Lists	Universe
Political	85	11,890	56	7,995	51.8	48.7
Nonpolitical	223	53,713	110	24,371	102.7	120.4
Fund raising merchandise and services	13	2,384	14	2,414	(7.1)	(1.2)
Total	321	67,987	180	34,780	78.3	95.5

CHAPTER 12

Transition: The Name of the Game

It would take a gift of clairvoyance to predict exactly what our direct marketing business will be like in the next decade. But one thing is certain: Advancing technology in the foreseeable future will reprogram every aspect of direct marketing. This will be a necessity because direct marketing is booming as more Americans opt for the convenience of home shopping. Industry studies have predicted that by 1990, half of all consumer goods will be purchased from the home. Farfetched? Perhaps, but even a lower percentage would serve as the catalyst for change.

DATA BASES AND NETWORKING

A major revolution will take place in the list business through data bases and networking. This could result in definitive markets—not lists.

For example, perhaps magazines in the intellectual and cultural field (*Harper's, Atlantic, Saturday Review, New Republic, Commentary,* etc.) might cooperatively appoint a representative to market a single unduplicated list of all intellectual magazine readers in the United States. (The regional magazines are already exploring this concept.)

The financial advisory services for years have been fishing out of the same barrel. With the proliferation of financial products, a nonduplicated master list of known and/or qualified investors seems to make sense for the future.

Will it happen? Possibly and probably. Personal computers can make this all possible. It's a given that computer companies have now decided that the real future of personal computers lies in business and that business will welcome networking.

The most realistic type of network will be a gathering of independently functional participants that can share information freely among any or all participants in the network, for example, list brokers with list managers and both with list owners. But the most important breakthrough will be list professionals online with their clients.

Insofar as list data bases are concerned, the value of this collective market approach is quite evident. And there are some already in place. However, there is a problem: the reluctance of many list owners to join a data base, understandably so in some instances. Their own house list is a *large* sophisticated data base. If they joined a data base, their list could represent 50 percent or so of the total quantity, and they would lose some measure of control. So why do it? Well, why not? When and if the benefits to the list owner can be precisely defined, we'll have an answer to the"why-not" question.

Another challenge will be the methodology used in the "collection of lists." Some of the current list data bases have an aura of homogeneity but are really not totally representative of a "homogenized" market. In order for this approach to be acceptable and successful, it will be necessary to build these data bases on the basis of not only a real market theme but also on the basis of quality and activity. The desire to build a large universe must take a backseat to these qualifiers and preclude the tendency to add names of inferior quality, for example, difference between buyers and inquiries, customers with no activity in a 12-month period versus recent or multiple activity, unit of sale, source, etc.

THE NEED FOR SPECIALIZATION

While some networking is already in place in our industry, the future does appear to lie in specialization. The data bank (synonymous with "data base") should allow calling for varied types of information but should be specialized just as cable TV channels are. You can call one data bank for recent stock quotes, another for legal news, another for sports news. The advantage is the fact that the latest news is available instantly and easily long before the same information is available in print. The disadvantage at this point is the cost.

Actually, in the investment field there already is a "stock screening" system. This involves using a computer to search through all the stocks in a data base to find those which relate to the individual's investment goals by giving the computer specified criteria. If the investor is interested in high-yield utilities, the computer should be instructed to find the stocks which yield over 6 percent, are in the utilities category, and have a low debt. Financial experts caution that screening alone should not serve as the final stock purchase decision but should be the starting point for research on the stocks which look promising.

A list data bank which requires numerous update entries can be expensive. In order to access the most current list information, frequent updates are required—quantity, state and Zip code counts, hotline, changes of address, unit of sale, etc.—which possibly could be provided to the participant via updated diskettes on a monthly basis.

However, of equal importance as the updating is the screening application. If you have access to a large data base with hundreds of bits of information, how will the subscriber use this information to screen the names before ordering? Of necessity, it would appear that the mailer would need to call up the information based on a predetermined set of criteria as described in the investment field application.

A CHALLENGING OPPORTUNITY

Networking in direct marketing is still in the embryo stage even though the value of networking—allowing computers to talk to each other—has already proven itself in other disciplines. The next step must be a thorough evaluation of the concept as a whole as it relates to direct mail promotions and a definitive evaluation of how best the process can be structured to serve the diverse companies which belong to the direct mail discipline. It is difficult, virtually impossible, to be "all things to all people." The market segment for any information system is a group of customers that needs a particular service (in this case, information) in the same format with the same discrete factors. If the need exists (and that's the crux of the matter), it will be done, but only if those of us in the service business—the segmenters—can identify and segment the needs of our constituency. A challenging opportunity.

LAST NOTE

From a historical point of view, it can be observed that advertising has drawn much of its form and content from the socioeconomic environment in which it was created. The "then," "now," and "tomorrow" have a constant: a prescribed direction. In order to be effective, the look, the feel, the message of advertising must relate to current trends—changing styles of life, sophisticated consumer attitudes, technology, legal and ethical considerations, plus other continuing external influencers.

At this time, there is recognition that the only continual occurrence in direct response marketing is *change*. There is also the recognition that each company has a laboratory of experience in-house which encompasses every discriminant function of direct response marketing. It is this "technostructure" that makes it possible to gather and use information, observe important trends, and attain greater efficiency on a continuing basis.

This data-driven approach will force a stratagem which is both anticipatory and adaptive, that is, a strategy away from *undifferentiated marketing*, which involves using the same approach to all customers, and *concentrated marketing* toward a single market, which is sometimes effective but can be self-limiting. The best approach will have to be *differentiated marketing*, that is, a method of developing different products and advertising approaches for clearly defined market entities.

In a booming direct marketing atmosphere, where it is projected that by 1990 a vast quantity of all consumer goods will be purchased from the home, the term "direct marketing" will be an oxymoron unless we harness, refine, and define our information to serve a basic business philosophy. That philosophy must be one of promoting our products and services only to those prospects most likely to respond.

CHAPTER 13

The Dimension of Privacy

Consider this statement in a letter from a prominent stock brokerage firm: "Our individual accounts are select and few, typically investors with $500,000 invested in securities and a net worth of at least $2,000,000. . . ."

This solicitation was followed up with a phone call. When the recipient expressed alarm that a stranger was aware of his financial standing and other personal demographic characteristics, the stockbroker hung up. It was later learned that this approach was dropped because of the invasion of privacy issue.

CONCERNS OF PRIVACY

In recent polls, it was found that the percentage of Americans who said they were "very concerned" about threats to privacy increased substantially. It appears that four Americans in five believe it would be easy for someone to assemble a master file on their lives that would violate their privacy.

The DMA's "Guidelines on the Use of Mailing Lists" suggests that there is certain personal information that the consumer *reasonably expects* will not be transferred to any other party. How would we, as consumers, like to have our exact income, net worth, investment transactions, medical records, death of a family member, etc. be made available on a list? We would object because we would consider these types of data private and confidential. And there is other personal data which consumers would consider private.

Suppose that the media jumped on the actual availability of lists of widows, individuals with physical disabilities, parents of retarded children, and so on. What do you think this would mean relative to the privacy issue?

All of us in the list business (and mailers too) must recognize these problems. They're real. Let's, on an individual basis, take action wherever we can to keep those types of lists off the market.

Then there is another side of the problem: the promotion by some list compilers in the consumer field. They don't always "tell it as it is." The message usually does not talk in terms of median or averages but in *absolutes*. They talk about characteristics such as age, sex, income, occupation, number of children, and type of dwelling, on an *individual* basis. While this information *may* be available on certain of these factors, there is doubt that age, occupation, income, and number of children are always available on an *individual* basis. Much is assumed or inferred based on a geographical measurement unit. *So, why not so state?* If the compiler has confidence that the methodology used has statistical validity, there is no need to oversell.

Let's be realistic. It isn't essential to know an individual's real income and/or net worth. If someone subscribes to a financial publication, a photography magazine, a fashion magazine, or a health publication, the subscription itself positions the person as a prospect for certain types of related products. As mentioned previously, lifestyle does add a humanizing element.

The DMA Privacy Task Force, which was in action about a decade or so ago, must have concern with the new currents about privacy. The question of mailing lists will arise as it did in 1974. Presently the specter of abuse extends to telephone marketing to interactive cable TV as well as to direct mail. Even though the use of mailing lists was not in the original Privacy Act of 1974, it became one of the principal concerns of Congress. The Privacy Protection Committee, headed by David Linowes, decided against including restrictions on mailing lists in the act because of the DMA's Mail Preference Service for Consumers which gives them the opportunity to be "delisted."

This self-policing was the fundamental factor which influenced the committee. And that is what the list business needs to address: a sensitivity to the consumer's right to privacy.

With the increasing concern about data bases which seem to imply invasion of privacy, the list community must do everything possible to recognize and address this concern. The truth is that list owners and compilers are *not* dossier compilers or personal investigators and shouldn't be. But in today's world, what one is, is often less important than what one is *perceived* to be. If there's one major challenge that needs to be addressed, it is to find an effective way to make sure that the public's perception of list rental is shaped *by us,* not the media. And not by those companies in our field that just don't care. When the media write that the more esoteric the criteria (people under 30 who own reptiles), the more expensive the list, it's discouraging. Somehow the message to the outside world about lists still hasn't overcome the inaccuracies fostered by list companies who oversell and the media which don't understand.

Look at these headlines which recently appeared in a variety of media:

Forum: One's Privacy Periled

A New Law that Will Truly Protect New Yorkers' Privacy

IRS Use of Mail-Order Lists

How Lives Can be Threaded for State Control

Creative Thought Needed to Cope with the Privacy Issues

Privacy Threats Worry Americans

IRS Starts Hunt for Tax Evaders Using Mail-Order Concerns' Lists

Electronic Mail a Threat to Privacy

Private Computers' Income Data to Aid IRS in Hunt for Evaders

Getting Off Mailing Lists Isn't Always Easy

Concern over Abuses in Data Collection (Data Base) Prompts House of Representative Hearings

"Junk" Mail? It may be just trash to you, but it's a $150 billion business

As long as headlines such as these keep appearing and list companies are willing to hype these messages, the problem will always be with us.

THE QUESTION OF ETHICS

Let's think in terms of our ethical responsibilities to the consumer, to our industry, to our company, and to ourselves by observing the following:

1. Always insist on a sample of the mailing piece from an unknown firm,
   and review it carefully.
2. If the offer (diamonds for 99 cents) appears ludicrous, do *not* allow
   usage of the list. This, obviously, also applies to cheap rip-offs of
   brand-name items, investment opportunities which promise a large
   and quick return, pornographic books and items, and any other ques-
   tionable services or products.

Let's get on with the Number 1 task: getting the direct marketing industry
off the Number 1 position on the list of complaints to the FTC.

THE ISSUE OF ETHICS

Everyone involved in the issue of privacy and other government
agency regulations must recognize that there is a turning point. Whatever
the feelings, the issue of privacy is not likely to change profoundly to our
benefit. If anything, it will be the other way. And those companies which
follow the rules of self-policing will accrue benefits to themselves as well as
to our disciplines: direct mail, phone, space, TV, cable, and radio. If this
issue is not addressed, the "onus of failure" can't be attributed to government agencies but to us. We must be professionally competent in dealing
not only with postal issues but with all the regulatory agencies: Federal
Trade Commission, Federal Communications Commission, the Council
of Better Business Bureaus, and the U.S. Postal Service. We must pay
close attention to mail-order rules, privacy issues, cable and interactive
regulations, telephone restrictions, and access to lists.

Throughout the business world, new attention is being paid to the
question of ethics. We can't afford not to be part of this effort.

All direct marketers must keep aware of legislative, litigative, and
regulatory developments. Problems that give rise to legislation are usually
legitimate, but the regulations do not always reflect the necessity. It is up
to our community to emphasize our self-regulatory efforts and to up-
grade the integrity and public image of direct response marketing.

CHAPTER 14

List
Security

The matter of list security has taken on some new dimensions in the last year or so, and the word "theft" has reared its ugly head. While the extent is open to question, there is no doubt that measures should be taken relative to the security of your names.

Some points which should be observed by list owners are:

1. List owners must communicate their concern about the possible unauthorized use of their list to their internal data processing center, their service bureau, or any unit that has access to the file.
2. Seeded names must be national in coverage and should be changed at least annually. Access to the seeded names should be limited and controlled. Only very responsible parties should have access to this file.
3. List owners should insist that "warning" labels be included on tapes to indicate that the list is decoyed, no copy is to be retained, and unauthorized use is illegal. (The owner's lawyer can expand this statement.) The same warning should be included with shipments of labels.
4. Even though it is recognized that a copy of the tape must be made in order to process a merge/purge, list owners should require the return of the magnetic tape to the address shown on the reel.

5. Magazines should always have an updated list of their authorized subscription agents which can be referenced by their fulfillment service.
6. Complaints received by subscribers about nonreceipt of magazines, billing, etc. should be carefully monitored. A substantial increase in such complaints could be a warning of unauthorized use of the list by subscription agents, particularly by telephone.
7. The seeded names should be advised that if they receive a telephone solicitation to renew, they should accept the offer and request that the solicitor submit an invoice. The invoice could be a source of information for unauthorized use.
8. The list owner should warn the seeds that if they respond to an offer they receive under the seeded name, they must change the name; otherwise it becomes part of another list and creates a "false" alarm.

MAILING LIST SECURITY PROGRAM

There are comprehensive measures that can be taken to limit the chances of mailing list theft. With special emphasis on name and address seeding, a step-by-step security program is detailed in Appendix 14A for companies who frequently rent out lists. A summary checklist provides criteria of evaluating a current list security program.

Mailing lists are a significant asset to organizations who use direct mail. A good list can be a major source of sales. Or the list itself, if rented, can be a direct source of revenue. As with other assets, however, mailing lists are subject to unauthorized use and outright theft. Therefore, security of mailing lists should always be of concern to management. Mailing lists can and must be protected with diligence on a continuing basis.

However, the security measures are different from those applicable to most other assets. For example, the value of lists cannot generally be assessed, and, therefore, insurance is not a viable hedge. In any case, insurance proceeds would be a small consolation if your list ended up in the hands of a competitor. In addition, data has a peculiar nature. It can be stolen, via copying, and still leave the owner in possession.

There are numerous methodologies which have been developed specifically related to list security. Appendix 14A represents one very viable approach.

APPENDIX 14A

Mailing List
Security Program

There are several facets to a good mailing list security program. For this article, I have divided these into the following six categories. Each will be explained in detail.
 I. Program Administration
 II. Ascertaining the Legal Environment
 III. Limiting Exposures
 IV. Marking the List
 V. Discouraging Theft
 VI. Maintaining Accountability

I. PROGRAM ADMINISTRATION

Two administrative steps are required to assure an adequate program. First, overall responsibility for the program should be assigned to a specific individual with secondary responsibilities assigned to security, data processing or marketing personnel as applicable. Secondly, the program should be reviewed periodically by a party with no direct responsibility for the program such as internal audit or an outside consultant.

II. ASCERTAINING THE LEGAL ENVIRONMENT

After assigning administrative responsibilities one of the first steps in establishing a list security program at a particular installation should be to investigate the legal environment. This environment can help determine which protective measures are appropriate. There will almost certainly be variances among countries.

The following two paragraphs summarize the legal environment in the U.S. as explained to me by legal counsel.

Copyrights and patents do not apply to mailing lists. Therefore, this avenue of protection is not available. Mailing lists are similar to trade secrets. They are confidential and proprietary.

There are two major concerns to keep in mind should legal action be required to recover or halt the unauthorized use of a misappropriated list. First, you must be able to prove that the property is yours. Secondly, you must be able to prove that reasonable protective measures have been taken.

Source: DMMA Manual Release #5310 "How to Institute an Efficient Mailing List Security Program" by Kenneth L. Emens. *DIRECT MAIL/MARKETING MANUAL DM/MA,* 6 East 43rd Street, New York, NY 10017.

III. LIMITING EXPOSURES

Limiting exposures is one of the aspects of a good security program. There are several elements involved.

Identification of Exposures

The first logical step in limiting exposures at a particular installation is to identify those exposures.

This would include identification of each medium the list occurs in, the physical locations, the size of the accumulation, frequency of availability, etc. The exposures can then be ranked to set the order for implementation of control procedures and protective techniques.

Any accumulation of names and addresses should be considered a list. These lists can exist in various forms—mailing labels; invoices; hardcopy lists; microfilm; computer tapes; disks and memory; manual records; files, etc. Lists should be protected in all forms.

The value of a particular accumulation is influenced by the size and quality of the list. For example a list of one hundred prime customers would be more valuable than a list of ten thousand deadbeats. Protective measures should vary accordingly.

Eliminating Unnecessary Exposures

The necessity of each exposure should be reviewed. Unnecessary exposures should be eliminated leaving only those where there is a business need. Some other measures which can be employed to limit exposures include:

1. Lock areas where lists are stored and limit access to authorized persons. This includes the computer room and storage areas for hardcopy, microfilm and magnetic tapes, etc.
2. Make sufficient and suitable secure cabinets available.
3. Physically lock lists up when not in use.
4. Do not display complete address information on internal lists and reports. The second and third address lines are critical for mailings but not usually required for in-house work.
5. Destroy lists as soon as they are no longer needed.
6. Shred or burn obsolete lists where possible.
7. Erase computer tapes, disks and memory when no longer needed.
8. Don't give lists in readable forms to refuse disposal organizations.
9. Require password control over computer and data file access.
10. Store data in coded form using cryptographic techniques.

IV. MARKING THE LIST

To seek recovery or injunctive relief should your list be stolen, it is necessary to prove that the list is your property. To prove this, your list must be marked in some manner.

Name and Address Modification

A list can be marked by placing unique, fictitious names and addresses in it. One approach commonly used is to misspell names in a unique manner. For example, my name and address is:

Kenneth L. Emens
38 Ridley Avenue
Aldan, PA 19018

The first line could be changed to Kenneth L. Emmens, K.Z. Emens, etc. to make the name unique.

However, placement of seed identifying data in the first line is not as good as the second or third line. First line data can be replaced randomly, rearranged, removed, or replaced with "Resident" or "Occupant." This would eliminate the uniqueness of the name and address without affecting mailability.

The second line can be "seeded" by using the technique described for the first line. In addition, other possibilities include:

1. Add a code behind the street address, e.g. 39 Ridley Ave. 18
2. Add a code in the second line disguised as an apartment number, e.g. 39 Ridley Ave., Apt. 18.

Completely Fictitious Seeds

Someone who stole your list could defeat the uniqueness of your seed in the above examples by scrambling and replacing letters and numbers on a random basis. Therefore, one of the best seeds is a completely fictitious person and/or address. This can be done by establishing a Post Office Box or using a non-existent street address. For example: Mickey Mouse, Box 99 or 139 Ridley Ave. where there is no 100 block. This might take a little cooperation from the local postmaster to open a Post Office Box in a fictitious name or from the postman to insure that mail to a non-existent address gets delivered properly.

List Dating

Seed identifying characteristics should be changed on a periodic basis. This allows a stolen list to be dated as well as identified. Such information can help establish who had access to the list.

For example: a seed could be set up with two initials and a surname such as A.A. Emens. The first initial could stand for a year (A = 1970, B = 1972, etc); the second initial could stand for a month (A = January, B = February, etc.) or a bi-weekly period.

Another way to date lists is to include a date in the seed name and/or address. For example, the last four digits of the current Julian date could be appended to a surname or disguised as an apartment number. Two examples of Julian dates for given Gregorian dates follow. 1/13/76 would be 76013, 2/15/75 would be 75046. If labels or a list were produced on 1/13/76 (Julian 76013), the last four digits could be placed in a seed name as an apartment number such as 39 Ridley Ave., Apt. 6013.

Other Aspects of a Good Seed Program

□ The number of seeds should be adequate to cover each logically expected subset, for example each mailing segment, reel of magnetic tape or microfilm cassette. There is no hard and fast rule in this regard. The quality of the seeds is more important than the quantity.

□ The seeds should be dispersed over the same geographic area as the list.
□ Some seeds should be identifiable and be included in all lists, labels and other outputs created. These seeds are a protection against outsiders and some insiders.
□ Automatic inclusion of the above seeds should be under computer program control if the list is computerized and be included in all mailings.
□ Some seeds should not be identifiable as such. They should appear to be normal in all aspects. This would include the purchase of product, maintaining of an account balance or whatever. These seeds are a protection against insiders.
□ The unidentified seeds should be maintained independently by at least two individuals. This would then necessitate collusion to obtain a totally seedless list.
□ A positive feedback loop must be established with the seeds. Records of mailing should be maintained. Seeds should be provided with return envelopes and instructed to return all mail received in the seed name. Return from seeds should be recorded and exceptions investigated.
□ Seeds should be tested from time to time by sending foreign or competitive literature to them under the seed name.

Likely Candidates for Seeds

Persons with an interest in the direct mail business and/or security probably make the best seeds. Likely candidates include contacts in the direct mail business, contacts of your security personnel, relatives and friends. (DMMA's Mail Monitor Service—Release #9110—can provide these seed names of interested direct marketers who have volunteered to provide this service to other DMMA members—free of charge.)

V. DISCOURAGING THEFT

Management should consistently display their concern for security in their words and actions. This should insure a top down security-conscious organization. Physical security precautions should be highly visible.

Knowledge of the presence of seeds should also discourage theft. Their presence can be communicated by an appropriate warning message such as:

WARNING
The names and addresses in files and lists have been seeded to detect unauthorized duplication.

This warning message can be stamped on lists and label runs, applied as stickers to magnetic tape reels or microfilm cassettes, posted as signs, etc. This applies to in-house lists and lists developed, maintained or released out-of-house.

Formal agreements with employees to hold company data confidential can also be effective preventives. The same type of proprietary information agreement should also be used with outside vendors who have access to your list.

Should a theft be committed and the thieves apprehended, vigorous prosecution should follow. This can serve as an example that you mean business in the area of protecting your list.

VI. MAINTAINING ACCOUNTABILITY

Where possible, accountability control of lists should be maintained. Each listing should be accounted for from its inception to ultimate disposition which is usually destruction or dispersion. Each change of hands should be fully documented and acknowledged with signature receipts. A sample of a list accountability control document is provided in Exhibit A. Additional elements in an accountability control system include:

1. Send copies of Accountability Control Documents to a central responsible person.
2. Extend the accountability control to persons outside the organization as necessary, for example, to mailing houses.
3. Disallow unauthorized copies.
4. Issue replacement/updated lists only upon the return of the outdated version.

CONCLUSION

No security system is 100% effective. However, in the area of mailing list security, there are a number of protective measures that can be taken to

Accountability Control Document			Serial No. 00986
Name of Document	Pages	Report no.	Date created
Form ☐ List ☐ Microfilm		☐ Magnetic tape	☐ Other
Received by	Date	Received by	Date
Destroyed by	Witnessed by		Date

Exhibit A

limit the probability of theft. There are also things that can be done to allow for recovery or injunctive action should a list be stolen and used without authority. When applied appropriately and collectively, these measures should provide an adequate degree of security.

MAILING LIST SECURITY CHECKLIST

This list was designed to assist in the evaluation of a mailing list security program. Negative answers generally indicate weak areas unless compensating measures are employed or the cost/benefit ratio is not favorable.

I. Program Administration
A. Has overall responsibility been assigned?
B. Have specific responsibilities been assigned?
C. Is the program reviewed by an independent party?

II. Ascertaining the Legal Environment
A. Has the legal environment been reviewed?
B. Have the actions required to recover or halt the use of a misappropriated list been identified?

III. Limiting Exposures
A. Have all storage mediums been identified?
B. Have all physical locations been identified?
C. Have the exposures been ranked?
D. Have unnecessary exposures been eliminated?
E. Are storage areas kept locked?
F. Is access limited to authorized persons?
G. Are sufficient secure cabinets available?
H. Are lists locked up when not in use?
I. Have second and third lines in names and addresses been suppressed where possible?
J. Are lists destroyed as soon as possible?
K. Are obsolete lists shredded, burned or otherwise destroyed?
L. Are lists destroyed before going to a refuse disposal organization?
M. Are computer tapes, disks and memory erased when no longer needed?
N. Are password controls employed over access to:
 1. computer?
 2. data files?
O. Are cryptographic techniques employed?

IV. Marking the list
A. Is the list seeded?
B. Are second and third lines of names and addresses seeded?
C. Are completely fictitious seeds used?
D. Are lists dated?
E. Is the number of seeds adequate to cover each expected subset?
F. Is the geographic coverage of seeds adequate?
G. Are some seeds included in all outputs?

H. Is seed inclusion under computer program control?
I. Are some seeds unidentifiable as such?
J. Are the unidentified seeds maintained independently by at least two individuals?
K. Is a positive feedback loop with seeds maintained?
L. Are seeds instructed to give prompt notification of receipt of unexpected mail?
M. Are the seeds tested?

V. Discouraging Theft
A. Does management display concern for security?
B. Are physical security precautions highly visible?
C. Is the presence of seeds openly communicated?
D. Are all lists, files, tape reels, etc. marked with a seed warning message?
E. Do employees have to sign confidentiality agreements?
F. Do vendors have to sign confidentiality agreements?
G. Are apprehended thieves prosecuted?

VI. Maintaining Accountability
A. Is a document accountability system maintained?
B. Does the system cover birth to death of each list?
C. Is each movement documented by signature receipt?
D. Is document destruction witnessed and documented?
E. Do copies of accountability control documents go to a central place?
F. Does the accountability control system extend outside the organization?
G. Are unauthorized copies disallowed?
H. Are replacement lists issued only upon return of the outdated version?

Glossary

Active buyer   Also described as "active customer." Usually one who has made a purchase within the last 12 months.

Active member   In book and record clubs, a member who is either fulfilling a commitment or who has fulfilled the commitment and is still purchasing.

Active subscriber   The live list of a magazine; the people who have ordered and paid for a subscription and are currently receiving the publication.

Alphanumeric   Pertaining to a character set that contains letters, digits, and sometimes other characters such as punctuation marks.

Back end   Persistency. This term refers to the measurement of customer activity after the initial order has been received. For example, with magazines, it would involve conversions and renewals.

Back test   Often described as a "retest" or "confirming test." For example, a list was tested with 10,000 names. The response was within an acceptable range but not good enough to order a large quantity. To reconfirm the results, a retest quantity of 15,000 to 20,000 was ordered. This schematic also applies to other tests such as offer, package, and price.

Bad pay   Also referred to as "nonpay." Subscription or membership offers which are "bill-me" (charge orders) and which subsequently must be cancelled due to nonpayment.

Batch processing   Refers to the sequential input of computer programs or data.

Behavioral research   A study of human behavior.

Binary   Relating to a system of numbers having 2 as its base using only the digits 0 and 1.

Bit   A binary digit; the smallest unit of information in a computer.

BPI(*bytes per inch*)   Bytes per inch on magnetic tape (see Tape density). A group of bits, usually eight, that stores a piece of information. Computer memory is measured in bytes: 32K means 32,000 bytes.

Breakeven   The point in a business transaction when income and expenses are equal.

Bulk mail   Same as third-class mail.

Bulk shipment   See Continuity program.

Buyer   Someone who has purchased from a company.

Buyers (1982 – 1984)   Indicates that these people purchased from the company at one time during one of these years.

Carrier route   Grouping of addresses based on the delivery route of each letter carrier. The average number of stops is 400 but does range from under 100 to 2500 to 3000. In total there are about 180,000 carrier routes in the United States.

Carrier route presort   Refers to presorting of mail (usually by a letter shop) to carrier route by Zip codes and preparing it to specifications established by the U.S. Postal Service. Properly executed, the mailing so prepared receives a discounted postal rate.

Cell(s)   In list terminology, a statistical unit or units. A group of individuals selected from the file on a consistent basis.

Central processing unit (CPU)   The unit within a computer system that has the circuits to control the execution of instructions.

Change of address (Chad and COA)   The process of changing an address on internal files upon notification from the customer. Also a selection offered by a list owner of people who moved within a recent period, usually 1 to 3 months.

Cheshire label   A continuous form on which names and addresses are printed in a special format (usually 4 across and 11 down). These labels must be processed by a Cheshire labeling machine which automatically cuts the paper into single labels and affixes each to an envelope, order card, or any vehicle which will be used to mail the piece.

Cluster   A number of similar persons grouped together to form a selection criteria for list selection and analysis, e.g., Zip codes can be clustered on a variety of demographic criteria or past performance.

COBOL   *Co*mputer *B*usiness *O*riented *L*anguage. A procedure-oriented business computer language.

CODE   See Key (number).

Commission   The fee paid to the list broker by the list owner for arranging the list rental transaction.

Compiled list   A list which is prepared from directories or other printed sources and from registrations at trade shows, conventions, etc.

Computer language   A generic term for the codes used to give computers instructions. Basic is a computer language.

Computer record   Information about an individual or company which contains all the transactional data.

Consumer behavior   The study of why consumers act as they do in buying or not buying. This research is used for marketing purposes.

Continuation   The next step after a list test. If the test proved responsive within established financial parameters, the list is reordered in quantities related to response.

Continuity program Books or any other service offered as a series of programmed purchases. For example, a continuity book program usually offers the first book free and the second and third books individually at a certain price. Upon receipt of payment for book 2 or 3, the balance of the volumes in the series are shipped at one time (bulk shipment). Also, products or services purchased as a series of small purchases, based on a common theme and shipped at specific predetermined intervals.

Control The promotion package which performs at an acceptable response level and is used for comparative purposes when other promotion packages are being tested.

Controlled circulation Recipients of a publication with a central theme. The publication is sent free of charge to a company where the type of company or occupational level of the recipient has been prequalified.

Co-op Two or more products or services (usually noncompetitive) mailed in one envelope to defined prospects.

Cost per order (CPO) An analytical tool based on an arithmetical formula which provides the exact amount it costs to secure the order. The formula varies from mailer to mailer, but the basics are pretty much the same (see Chapter 5).

Cost per thousand (CPM) The total promotional cost per thousand pieces of direct mail frequently referred to as "in the mail costs." Includes cost of the package, list, merge/purge, letter shop, and postage. *Example:* If the total cost is $20,000 and the mailing quantity is 100,000, then the cost per thousand equals $200 (that is, 100,000 ÷ $20,000 = $200).

CRT Cathode ray tube used for display of computer information, that is, a television tube used to display pictures or characters.

Customer profile A list of the key characteristics of customer segments.

Data A representation of facts, concepts, or instructions in a formal manner suitable for communication, interpretation, or processing by persons or automatic means.

Data base An integrated body of information. In direct marketing, an effective data base system must be application-oriented to meet user needs.

Debug To locate and correct defects (to debug a computer program).

Decoy name Unique name especially inserted into a mailing list to track list usage and in some instances to track the time it took for the postal system to deliver the mail.

Demographics The statistical characteristics of subpopulation groups with reference to age, income, occupation, etc. and with reference to size, density, and distribution.

DMA Direct Marketing Association. The primary trade association for direct marketers.

DMA Mail Preference Service See Mail Preference Service.

Dummy name See Decoy name.

Dupe Appearance of a name more than one time in the merge/purge process.

Dupe elimination (merge/purge) A system which matches names with a specific match code in order to retain the name only one time on the mailing file.

Exchange An arrangement where two mailers exchange quantities of names rather than renting. There are various reasons why this is done, e.g., some lists are available only on exchange such as nonprofit associations and when competitive products are involved.

Expire A magazine subscriber who did not renew a subscription.

Field A specified area used for a particular category of data in a computer record.

File maintenance "File" is another name for a list. See List cleaning.

Fortran *For*mula *Trans*lation. Computer language usually used to perform mathematical procedures.

Frequency Number of times a customer has purchased.

Front end Initial response to a mailing.

Fulfillment A critical aspect of direct marketing which refers to the processing and servicing of incoming orders.

Geo code Symbols used for the identification of geographic entities (state, county, city, Zip code, SCF, tract, etc.).

Grid A network of uniformly spaced horizontal and perpendicular lines. In direct mail, a test grid might resemble the following table:

Hardware Physical computer equipment as opposed to computer programs.

Hotline Refers to a recent transaction probably within the last 30 to 90 days.

House lists Internal files owned by a company.

	Package A	Package B	Package C	Total
List A	30,000	30,000	30,000	90,000
List B	30,000	30,000	30,000	90,000
List C	30,000	30,000	30,000	90,000
	90,000	90,000	90,000	270,000

Indicia Imprinted on the outgoing envelope to denote payment of postage.

Information retrieval The methods and procedures used to recover specific information from stored data.

Inquiries Involve people who requested a catalog, brochure, or more information.

Insert Refers to a promotional piece inserted into an outgoing package or invoice. Also described as a "package insert," or "billing stuffer."

Interface Connecting devices; where two or more independent systems meet and interact with each other as the interface between a computer and a printer.

Key (number) A unique unit of letters or numbers used on the reply device as an identifier to measure response from each list or list segment used in a direct mail campaign. Also used for other tests such as package or price. This technique is also used in other direct response media.

Letter shop The service company which labels and inserts promotional material into outgoing envelopes and sorts direct mail for delivery to the post office.

Lifetime value A measurement of the long-term dollar value of a customer, subscriber, donor, etc. This figure is essential when evaluating initial cost to bring in a customer against the lifetime proceeds.

List broker In very simple terms, the company which arranges for one company to use another company's mailing list. (Further details in Chapter 2.)

List cleaning The process by which a mailing list is kept up to date with address corrections, input of new names, and elimination of old names within specific time frames (monthly, quarterly, etc.). Also referred to as "list update."

List compiler A company or individual who develops lists of names and addresses from directories and other printed sources of consumers or businesses with common characteristics.

List exchange See Exchange.

List manager The inside unit of a list owner responsible for the marketing and promotion of the house list. An individual or company which serves the list owner as exclusive representative and is responsible for promotion and marketing, list clearance, record keeping, and collections.

List owner The company which owns a mailing list. Most list owners do rent and/or exchange their mailing lists upon approval of a mailing piece and clearance of a specific mail date (see Chapter 3).

List rental Refers to the rental of a list to a mailer for one-time use only for a specific promotion to be mailed on a specific date (see Chapter 3).

List segment Portions of a list which have been segregated based on definable criteria such as unit of sale, recency, frequency, gender, source, geographics, demographics, and other important characteristics.

List sequence The arrangement in which the names and addresses are kept in a file. Most lists today are filed in Zip code sequence and alphabetically by name within the Zip code. Some are in carrier route (postal delivery) sequence.

List source The media used to acquire names: direct mail, space, TV, radio, telephone, etc.

List test A random sample selected from a list to determine whether or not the list is responsive on a particular offer. Test quantities run from 5000 to 25,000 depending on the objective of the test (see Chapter 9).

M Refers to a 1000 measurement unit.

Magtape or magnetic tape A storage medium for electronically recording and reproducing computer-defined bits of data.

Mail date The date agreed to by a list user (mailer) and a list owner for a particular promotion.

Mail date protection The amount of time reserved by the list owner before and after the mail date assigned to a particular mailer by the list owner. For example, if a company is mailing an entire list, on, say, July 16, then the list owner agrees not to rent the list to any other mailer the week before or after the mail date.

Mailer The company which mails its promotion to a rented list.

Mail Preference Service This is a list of people who have contacted DMA to request that their names be deleted from all mailing lists.

Match code The identifier used to access a specific record on a file and also used to identify duplicates among lists. Actually, it is an abbreviation of the data on the file. For example, some of the criteria used are: (1) Zip code, city, and state, (2) first initial of first name, (3) full last name, or (4) address.

Members Denotes an active record or book club member or a credit card holder.

Menu In a computer program, a list of the types of functions which a user can choose at any time.

Merge/purge A system used to merge two or more lists in order to identify and eliminate duplication.

Multibuyers A customer who has bought more than one time from the same company within a preestablished time frame. Also referred to as "multiple buyer" or "repeat buyer."

Multihits A name that is matched more than once in the merge/purge process.

Multimedia   The use of a variety of media in promotional efforts such as direct mail, space, TV, or radio.

Negative option   A purchase plan in which a customer or member receives an advance notice at regular intervals about books or some other products which will be shipped to the customer unless the customer advises the company within a reasonable time frame not to ship.

Net-name arrangement   An agreement whereby the list owner agrees to accept payment for less than the quantity shipped, normally to compensate for duplicate names removed in the merge/purge process.

Nixie   An incorrectly addressed mailing piece returned to the sender by the U.S. Postal Service.

Nth-name sample   A numerical extraction from a list for testing purposes. For example, in an every-tenth-name sample, the first, eleventh, twenty-first, etc. names used would be used.

Offer   Refers to the specific product or service being promoted. Also refers to the terms under which it is being offered.

One-time use   A basic condition of list rental and exchanges. The names furnished can be used only one time. No copy can be retained.

Order card   The reply device used by the recipient to place an order by mail.

Package   Refers to the total elements assembled in a direct mail promotion.

Package test   A test of an entirely new solicitation or a test of one or more components of one mailing piece versus another. Usually measured against the control.

Paid inquiries   Prospects who paid to receive a catalog, brochure, or additional information.

Penetration   The percentage of names on a list in relation to a total, i.e., Zip code, households, etc.

Personalization   The addition of a name or other information about a prospect which is included in the copy, usually via computer.

Pressure-sensitive label   A label which is self-adhesive and attached to a backing sheet which is applied to the mailing piece. The intent here is to make it easier for the recipient to peel off the label and attach it to the return document.

Prospects   In direct mail, the names of people on a specific mailing list considered to be potential customers based on the characteristics of the list. Also can be compiled from directories or derived in the same manner as inquiries. In the case of industrial mailers, also by outside salespeople.

Psychographics   A study of lifestyle characteristics.

Random sample   A name chosen from a set which has an equal chance of being chosen as any other name in the set.

Rate-of-return curve   Refers to studies conducted by mailers to determine at which point in time a certain percentage of response (from a mailing) has been received which allows for accurate forecast of total response.

Referral   Usually derived from the Member-Get-A-Member technique, where a member is offered a record or book to suggest the names of five friends who might be interested in joining the club. Or, for example, in the case of a newsletter or magazine, a subscriber submits the names of five friends who will then receive a sample copy of the newsletter or magazine. These referral names are then solicited for full subscription or membership efforts.

Regression   A mathematical technique which produces a functional relationship between two or more correlated variables that is often empirically determined from data and is used especially to predict values of one variable when given values of the others.

Repeat mailing   A follow-up mailing, with a special promotion, to the same names within a month to 6 weeks after the first mailing. Also refers to a list which is mailed again within a certain period but not identified as a follow-up mailing.

Reply device   See Order card.

Response deck   A group of promotional postcards with reply capabilities, included in a mailing device, sent to a group of defined prospects.

Response rate   Results of a direct mail promotion as calculated in terms of the number of orders received divided by the total quantity mailed. This evaluation is one of the determinants used for lists and is therefore extremely important.

Return date   The date on which the mailer needs the names.

Return on investment (ROI)   The evaluation of return on invested capital. In direct mail, often loosely described as the return (income) based on the dollars expended in a direct mail campaign.

Return percent   Results of a direct mail promotion (see Response rate). Also used to identify the return of merchandise.

Running charge   The price charged by list owners for names not used as a result of removal of duplicates or cancellation of the order before the mail date.

Salt name   See Decoy name.

Sample mailing piece   The submission of the actual promotion package to a list owner for approval.

SCF count   Number of names in a given list for each Sectional Center Facility (SCF) code.

Sequence   An arrangement of names on a file according to a specified set of rules, for example, Zip code sequence.

Sex selection   The ability to select names by gender.

Shipping date   The date on which the list owner ships the names to the mailer.

Software   A set of computer programs and procedures.

Sort   To arrange data elements in an ordered sequence. Also to arrange mail in the sequence required for delivery by the postal service.

Source   Media used to acquire the names.

Split test   The use of two or more representative samples from the same list. Split tests are effective in testing package, offer, and/or price.

State count   Number of names in a given list for each state.

Tag   To mark a record with definitive criteria which allows for subsequent selection or suppression.

Tape density   Number of bytes included in each unit of magnetic tape [800 BPI (Bytes per inch)].

Tape dump   Data printout on magnetic tape used to check readability, consistency, etc.

Tape format (layout)   The arrangement and structure of data in a file including the sequence and size of its components. A map of the data included in each record and its specific location.

Test   See List test.

Test panel   Refers to the selection of names to be used in testing offers, packages, etc.

Test tape   A magnetic tape which identifies the format in which the names will be supplied.

Third-class mail   A class of mail which qualifies for reduced rates because of delayed handling by U.S. Postal Service. First- and second- class mail are handled first. One restriction is that each piece must weigh less than 16 oz. The rates are differentiated by the level of sorting. The postal service has a manual which details all the requirements.

Title addressing   Usually refers to functional titles used on compiled business lists where there is no individual name, for example, Attention: Personnel Director, ABC Company. Also can designate personal prefixes such as Mr., Ms., Mrs., or Doctor.

Trial subscribers   Someone who subscribes to a magazine or newsletter under a special short-term offer, for example, 3 months at $5 instead of 1 year at $20.

Unique names   After merge/purge, the names that will be mailed excluding all duplicates.

Universe   The total quantity of a mailing list. Also the total quantity available in a market—i.e., people interested in photography.

Update   See List cleaning. In addition, "update" also means adding current transactional data to each record on the list.

USPS   United States Postal Service.

Zip code   A numerical code assigned to geographical areas by the U.S. Postal Service (USPS). The first three digits represent a USPS sectional center facility or major post office. The last two digits represent delivery areas served by the branches of the major post office.

Zip code sequence   The arrangement of a list according to the numeric progression of Zip codes. From Zip code 01001 (Agawam, Massachusetts) to Zip code 99926 (Annette, Alaska). This arrangement includes every record on the file and is mandatory for mailing at bulk third-class rates based on the sorting requirements of USPS regulations.

Zip count   Number of names in a given list for each Zip code.

Index

ABOUT THE AUTHOR

Rose Harper, President, CEO, and coarchitect of Kleid Company, Inc., list consultants, New York, has had a long and highly successful career in direct mail marketing. She is the first woman to have been elected both treasurer and chairperson of the DMA. She served on the DMA Board Committee that developed the Mailing List Guidelines. In 1985 she was elected to the Direct Marketing Hall of Fame (the first woman to receive this honor) and she received the Silver Apple Award from the Direct Marketing Club of New York.

Currently she serves on the board of DMA and is chairperson of the DMA Strategic Planning Committee. She also serves on the board of trustees of the DMA Educational Foundation and the advisory board of New York University Center for Direct Marketing.

Her speeches, presentations, and articles have appeared in *Direct Marketing* magazine, the DMA *Fact Book*, and the DMA *List Monograph*. She was written up in *Mail Order Know-How* by Cecil C. Hoge, Sr.